- STUDENT WORKBOOK -

THE JOURNEY
divorce through the eyes of a teen

Unless otherwise indicated, all scriptural references have been taken from the New International Version (NIV) of the Bible, which is published by Zondervan Corporation, Grand Rapids, Michigan (parent company: Harper-Collins Publishers, New York). Used by permission. All rights reserved. Scriptures marked (TLB) are taken from The Living Bible.

Typeset design by Jane Tokar

Illustrations by Bridget Opdahl

Copyright © 2007, 2010, 2017 by Krista Smith. All rights reserved.

No part of this publication may be reproduced, transmitted, transcribed, stored in a retrieval system, or translated into any language, in any form or by any means, electronic, mechanical, or otherwise, without prior written permission from the author. No copy or reproduction shall be made, in whole or in part, without the express permission in writing from the author except as provided by USA copyright law.

This curriculum is not intended to be used as a replacement for psychologists or other health-care professionals. It is designed to be an additional resource to assist in the healing process. If further help is needed, please refer individuals to a psychologist, counselor, or health-care professional.

Any products or companies mentioned herein, whether or not accompanied by a trademark, registered trademark, or service mark, are the properties of their respective companies.

Printed in the United States of America.

Publishing services by Selah Publishing Group, Bristol, TN. The views expressed or implied in this work do not necessarily reflect those of Selah Publishing Group.

ISBN: 978-1-58930-307-2
LCCN 2017912516

Student Workbook
Table of Contents

Week 1 – The Roller Coaster of Grief 13

Week 2 – Step by Step 23

Week 3 – Getting a Grip 33

Week 4 – Hurts Band-Aids Can't Heal 43

Week 5 – Who Am I? 57

Week 6 – Where Is God When It Hurts? 65

Week 7 – Feelings Tune-up 75

Week 8 – Between Two Worlds 95

Week 9 – When One Becomes Two 109

Week 10 – The Missing Link 119

Week 11 – The End of the Journey 131

Week 12 – Hope On the Horizon 139

WELCOME TO *THE JOURNEY*

I'm glad you're here... I'm sad you're here.

This is one of the hardest things you will have to go through. I remember well when I had to tell my own children that their dad and I were separating. They were so sad. Their worlds had just blown up around them, and they had no control over anything that was happening. When they were with me, they missed their dad. When they were with their dad, they missed me. Nothing in their little world has been the same from that moment on. It's been over twenty years since that time, and I have watched how that decision between their dad and me has affected them every day of their lives. While watching my children go through my divorce, my heart began to break for all the children who have experienced the pain of losing the security of being raised in a two-parent home, which is why I decided to write *The Journey; Divorce Through the Eyes of a Teen,* with the hopes of making a difference in the lives of teens.

Being a teen is tough enough, but adding your parents' breakup to your already crazy world can be just about too much to handle. Your initial response may be to throw yourself into your friends, school, sports, or anything you think will distract you from the pain and other negative feelings you may be experiencing. But I would like to challenge you to take a different road, one that promotes healing and a promising future. I challenge you to go beyond what comes naturally and strive for wholeness, both for today and for your future.

If you do decide to take this challenge, I congratulate you! It will be a decision that will impact your life and change your future. I promise you that you will not regret it—and it will be fun along the way. If you decide not to dive in and work through the pain and confusion, research guarantees you will be putting a temporary lid on your pain and it will come out in other destructive ways as you grow older. Many young adults experience lives full of depression with little hope for a healthy future because they chose to ignore their pain earlier. I pray that will not be you.

In this Student Workbook, you will find worksheets that will promote healthy processing and offer tools to find peace in the midst of challenges. At the end of every session you will also find a Taking It Home section. This will be your homework for the week. It will consist of three parts–

Toward Yourself–Looking Inward
Toward Others–Looking Outward
Toward God–Looking Upward

The extent of your progress during these twelve weeks will rely mostly on whether or not you do these exercises and apply what you've been learning to your unique personal situation. At the beginning of every week, your leader will review a few of the questions, so please come prepared!

I highly encourage you to get involved and fully participate in all of the mixers and activities every week. It is a great opportunity to get to know people who are going through the same things you are. The more effort you put into these activities, the more you'll experience and gain new friendships throughout the process.

At the completion of these twelve weeks, my prayer is that you will have learned the tools you need to help you work through any situation that may come your way. I trust you will gain new friends to walk beside you and encourage you through this process, but my greatest prayer is that you will have gone deeper in your relationship with Christ. What I have learned from my own personal journey filled with unexpected challenges and unplanned pain, is that more than anything, without Him, complete healing is impossible.

You have your whole life ahead of you. Your future does not need to be defined by what is happening in your life now. Take control of your future by pressing through your current circumstances. My hope is that your life will be full of love, laughter, promise, and peace. Do not lay aside all that you've discovered through this program. Use these tools, with God's help, to create the future of your dreams.

I believe in you. God believes in you. Your leaders believe in you. Your friends believe in you. The question is–Do you believe in yourself? Step out in faith. God will see you through. A future of hope is out there. It's worth the effort to find it.

Thank you for sticking with it, even when things get tough. Remember, good things never come easy. Thanks for doing the hard work. You will not regret it.

With His grace,
Krista Smith-Larson

Steps to Peace with God

life question

How can I find peace?

Step 1 – God's Purpose: Peace and Life

God loves you and has a purpose for your life. God wants you to experience the life He created you to have. He wants you to have peace and purpose through a personal relationship with Him.

The Bible Says –

" We have peace with God through our Lord Jesus Christ. *Romans 5:1*

For God so loved the world that he gave his one and only Son, that whoever believes in him shall not perish but have eternal life. *John 3:16*

I have come that they may have life, and have it to the full. *John 10:10* "

life question

Why don't most people have the peace and purpose that God planned for us?

Step 2 – Our problem: The Missing Link

There's a problem, we know something is missing...an emptiness we can't seem to fill. We were created to have a relationship with God, but He did not make us to automatically have that need met. He gave us a will and the freedom to choose.

From the very beginning we were born as sinners. We chose to disobey God and run our own life. This is what the Bible calls sin. The result of living in sin is an empty life separated from God.

The Bible Says –

" All have sinned and fall short of the glory of God. *Romans 3:23*

The wages of sin is death, but the gift of God is eternal life in Christ Jesus our Lord. *Romans 6:23* "

life question
How can I reach God?

Step 3 – Solution: Realize there is only one way to reach God.

People try to fill the emptiness in their lives in many ways. They also try to build a bridge to God by doing a lot of good things.

The Bible Says —

He saved us, not because of righteous things we had done, but because of his mercy. *Titus 3:5*

There is a way that appears to be right, but in the end it leads to death. *Proverbs 14:12*

life question
How does God reach me?

Step 4 – God's Bridge: The Cross

Jesus provided the only way to God.

In order to bridge the gap between God and people, God sent His one and only Son, Jesus Christ, into this world. He died for our sins on the cross and conquered sin by being raised from the grave. This opened the way to forgiveness and a new relationship with God

The Bible Says —

But God demonstrates his own love for us in this: While we were still sinners, Christ died for us. *Romans 5:8*

Jesus answered, "I am the way and the truth and the life. No one comes to the Father except through me." *John 14:6*

Christ died for our sins according to the Scriptures...he was buried, and he was raised on the third day according to the Scriptures. *1 Corinthians 15:3-4*

life question

He did this for even me?

Step 5 – Our Response: Receive Christ

God has done everything necessary to provide forgiveness and restore the missing relationship in our lives. He offers us the choice to accept it. We accept it by trusting in what Jesus did for us on the cross and receiving Him as the Lord and Savior of our life.

The Bible Says –

Here I am! I stand at the door and knock. If anyone hears my voice and opens the door, I will come in and eat with that person, and they with me. *Revelation 3:20*

Yet to all who did receive him, to those who believed in his name, he gave the right to become children of God. *John 1:12*

If you declare with your mouth "Jesus is Lord," and believe in your heart that God raised him from the dead, you will be saved. *Romans 10:9*

Will you turn to Jesus Christ and receive Him right now?

1. Admit your need. *(I am a sinner. I've been running my own life.)*
2. Be willing to turn from your sin and make better choices.
3. Trust that Jesus Christ died for you on the cross and rose from the grave.
4. Invite Jesus Christ to come into your life and lead you in a new relationship with God. *(Receive Him as your Lord and Savior.)*

How to pray –

Dear Lord Jesus,
I know I am a sinner, and I ask for Your forgiveness. I believe You died for my sins and rose from the dead. I turn from running my own life, and now I ask You to run it. I invite You to come into my heart and life. I trust and follow You as my Lord and Savior. In Your name, Amen.

Signature _____

Date _____

The Bible Says —

Everyone who calls on the name of the Lord will be saved. *Romans 10:13*

For it is by grace you have been saved through faith, and this is not from yourselves, it is the gift of God, not by works, so that no one can boast. *Ephesians 2:8-9*

When you receive Christ, you are forgiven and placed in a new relationship with God as His child, through the supernatural work of the Holy Spirit, who now lives in you. This is what the Bible calls being "born again."

This is just the beginning of a wonderful new life in Christ. To grow in your new relationship with God, you should:

1. Read the Bible every day. Start with the gospel of John in the New Testament.
2. Talk with God through prayer. Communication is essential to a good relationship.
3. Join with others who worship, fellowship, and serve Christ in a church that teaches about Jesus.
4. Live for Christ by letting Him guide your life every day.
5. Tell others about how they can have peace with God. Pass on what you learned.
6. Demonstrate your new life by your love and concern for others.

⚠ This Is Our Safety Park!

- There are no wrong answers and no wrong feelings.
- There will be absolutely no making fun of people!
- You are free and encouraged to share any feelings you are experiencing.
- Everyone will be accepted for who they are and how they feel.
- We take turns. Everyone has a chance to speak and be heard.
- When others are sharing, you are listening.
- There will be no roughhousing allowed. We treat others with respect.
- There will be no PDA (Physical Displays of Affection) allowed. This is time to focus on you.
- Please refrain from using vulgar or offensive language.
- Commit to finding time for the "Taking It Home" assignments. This is where the difference will start to take place in your life.
- Cell phones must be put away and not used. We need to limit distractions and respect other's processing.
- What is shared with the group stays with the group.

HELPING CHILDREN DEAL WITH GRIEF

The Five Stages of Grief

- **DENIAL** — *This can't be happening.*
- **ANGER** — *Why is this happening to me?*
- **BARGAINING** — *I would do anything to change this.*
- **DEPRESSION** — *What's the point of going on?*
- **ACCEPTANCE** — *It's going to be ok.*

Grief: Keen mental suffering or distress over affliction or loss; sharp sorrow; painful regret
Dictionary.com

Scripture References

Is. 26:3	Jn. 14:1
Is. 41:10	Jn. 14:18
Is. 43:2	Jn. 14:27
Is. 46:9-10	Jn. 16:33
Is. 49:13	Rom. 8:18
Is. 53:4	2 Cor. 1:3-4
Jer. 31:13	2 Th. 2:16-17
Lm. 3:31-33	
Mt. 5:4	Heb. 4:16
Mt. 11:28	1 Pt. 5:6-7
Lk. 6:21	Rev. 21:4

GRIEF...A HEALING PROCESS We live in a culture that avoids grief. Oftentimes this leads to wanting to shelter children from grief, but nothing could be less helpful to a grieving child. While not pleasant, grief is a necessary process for kids processing any kind of loss. Whether the grief be from the death of loved one, change in family structure, loss of a pet or loss of friends, children need to go through the hard work of grieving in order to move on with their lives. You can help by walking the child through the process of grief and not trying to push or pull them through. Grief takes time, but it takes longer to repair the damage from unprocessed grief.

What To Say/Do

- "I am so sorry for your loss."
- "It's ok to cry."
- "What do you miss most?"
- "I don't know what to say, but I'm here for you."
- "Let's go get ice cream."
- "I wish I had the right words, just know that I care."
- "You'll be in my thoughts and prayers."
- Say nothing, just be there.

What NOT To Say/Do

- "I know how you feel."
- "God has a reason for everything."
- "God never gives us more than we can handle. How are you doing?"
- "You have to be strong for _____."
- "Time heals all wounds."
- "Be positive."
- "It's time to put this behind you."
- "If you think this is bad, _____."
- "Let me tell you about my loss."

http://Hope4HurtingKids.com

© 2017

The Roller Coaster of Grief

**Lesson One
Week 1**

GOALS

This week we want to:
1. Get to know one another
2. Be introduced to *The Journey*
3. Understand the Safety Park Guidelines
4. Get to Know Each Other
5. Introduce the Stages of Grief
    - Denial
    - Anger
    - Bargaining
    - Depression
    - Forgiveness
    - Acceptance
6. Complete the Attitude Check
7. Explain the Taking It Home sections

Verse of the week:

There is no fear in love. But perfect love drives out fear, because fear has to do with punishment. The one who fears is not made perfect in love.

1 John 4:18

Be Blessed!

May the Lord direct your hearts into God's love and Christ's perseverance.

2 Thessalonians 3:5

SOMETHING TO THINK ABOUT

We are glad you are here! For the next twelve weeks we will explore a variety of emotions, attitudes, and reactions you may have felt or expressed as a result of your parents' separation or divorce. We realize that it is not an easy time in your life, but our hope is that this group will be both a resource and an outlet for you to learn and grow from this unfortunate experience.

We encourage you to be open and honest as we set out on this journey together. Our prayer for you in this session is that God will give you a deeper understanding of the pure and passionate love He has for you.

The stages of grieving is not an easy subject, but it is a necessary first step on our journey…so let's get started.

Divorce Stats

YOU ARE NOT ALONE!
During your generation, over ____ of all teenagers will live in a broken home at some time in their lives.

Approximately ____ ____ children in the nation today are growing up without a father in their home, a total of ____. Over ____ more children live without a mother.

A couple marrying for the first time today has a lifetime divorce risk of over ____.

There are now more than ____ unmarried couples living together in the USA, a ____ increase since 1990. If these couples marry, these relationships are proven to have a higher divorce rate, of which ____ will have children.

Children from divorced families account for:

____ of youth suicides.
____ of pregnant teenagers.
____ of the homeless and runaway children.
____ of the institutionalized juveniles.

____ of children with behavioral disorders.
____ of all rapists.
____ of all high school dropouts.
____ of all adolescents in chemical abuse centers.
____ of all youths in prison.

All statistics from 2015 US Census Bureau and 2016 US Divorce Rates and Statistics Census

Family Definitions

Fill in the letter for each definition.

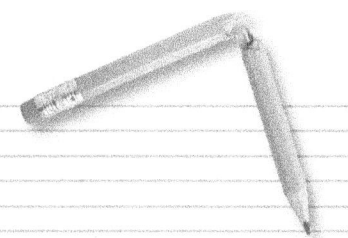

____ Joint Physical Custody   A. A family where a separation and/or divorce has taken place and your parents live in different homes

____ Single Parent Family   B. A family where divorce has happened and one or both of your parents have remarried

____ Custody   C. The parent who has physical custody of you

____ Custodial Parent   D. A court order allowing your parents to live separate and apart wile remaining legally married

____ Legal Separation   E. The parent who doesn't have physical custody of you

____ Birth or Biological Family F. The non-custodial parent's time with you

____ Half Brother/Sister   G. Money that the non-custodial parent pays to the custodial parent to go towards your expenses

____ Visitation   H. The legal termination of a marriage

____ Legal Custody   I. A family that consists of a birth father, a birth mother, yourself, and any biological siblings

____ Divorce   J. The day-to-day rights and responsibilities associated with raising you in their home and being responsible for your care and upbringing

____ Split Custody

____ Mediation   K. An informal process of resolving disputes that involves using a trained, neutral person, called a mediator, who seeks to bring the parties together to a mutually satisfying agreement

____ Non-custodial Parent   L. The sharing, of both parents, of the right to make important decisions about your welfare

____ Joint Legal Custody   M. The sharing, by both parents, of the actual physical care and custody of the children

____ Child Support   N. Parents' rights to the children

____ Physical Custody   O. The right to make important decisions about raising you, on issues such as health care, religious upbringing, education, etc.

____ Bended Family, or Stepfamily

                                P. A form of custody in which some or one of the children are in the custody of one parent and the remaining children are in the custody of the other parent

                                Q. A sibling related through one parent only

Attitude Check ✓

What is your "Grief Belief"?

Circle True or False for each statement below

1. People only feel grief when someone dies.	True	False
2. If you replace a loss (with a pet, girlfriend, etc.), your grief will go away.	True	False
3. You have to feel grief in order to move on.	True	False
4. Grief eventually ends.	True	False
5. Keeping super-busy can help you get through grief.	True	False
6. Expressing your grief should only be done in private.	True	False
7. When someone is expressing grief, you should leave him/her alone.	True	False
8. Grieving usually lasts one year.	True	False
9. It is okay to feel anger when you are grieving.	True	False
10. Everyone in your family will grieve the same way.	True	False
11. Once you graduate and leave your home, you will no longer grieve.	True	False
12. An effective way to grieve is to push your feelings away.	True	False

The Roller Coaster of Grief

Where are you on the Roller Coaster of Grief?
Put an "X" on the slope where you think you are.

Denial- Ignoring a situation in hopes it will go away

Anger- An expression of frustration over circumstances beyond your control

Bargaining- Offering a deal to get what you want

Depression- When you have given up and you feel like you have no hope

Forgiveness- Letting go of the past wrongs and moving on

Acceptance- The feeling that you can live with reality and be just fine

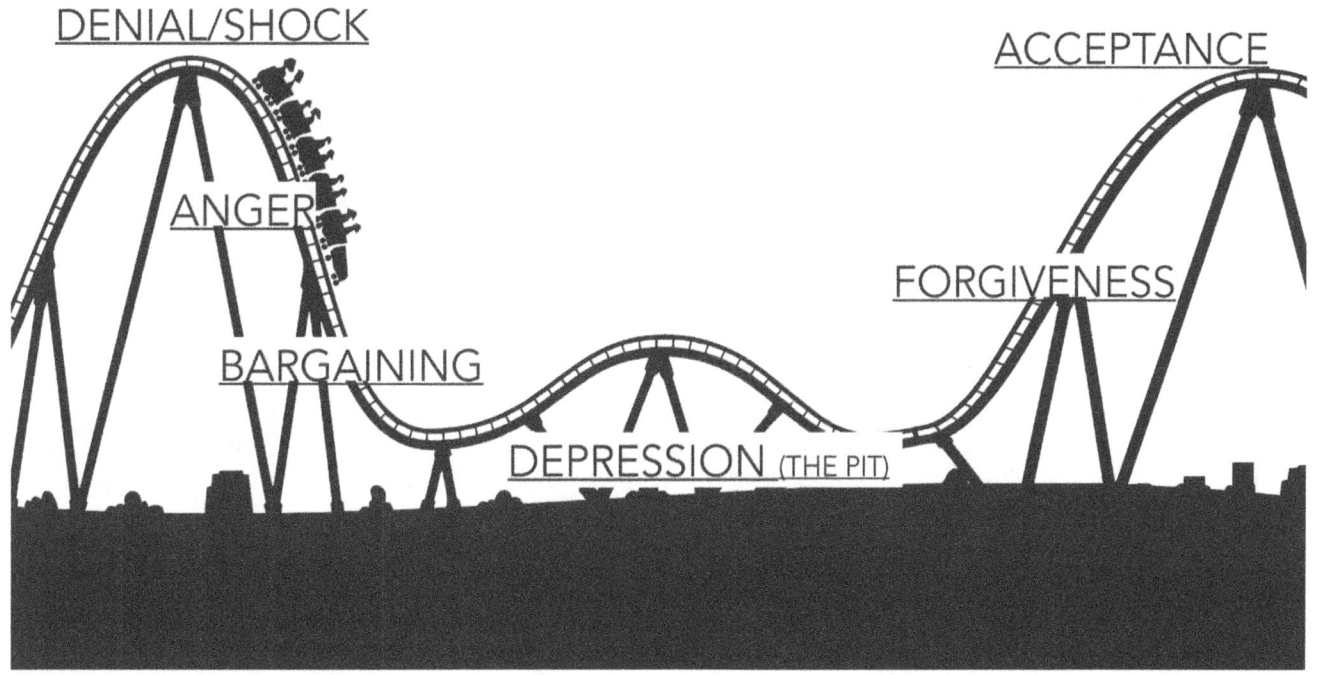

If I Could...

If I could live anywhere in the world, I would live...

If I could change one thing about my life, it would be...

If I could change one thing in the world, I would change...

If I could change one thing in my visitation schedule, it would be..

If I could have one wish come true, it would be...

If I could say one thing to one of my parents, I would say...

If I could be The President of the United States for one week, one thing I would change about the world in that one week is...

If I could do anything with my mom or dad, I would want to...

If I could choose only one meal to eat every day for the rest of my life, it would be...

If I could play any sport professionally, I would choose to play...

Taking It Home
Toward Yourself... Questions to take to my heart:

Look into your heart as you answer these questions. This is introspection time — time to grapple with what drives your thinking and behavior. Be sure to "capture your thoughts."

When you first found out your parents were separating/divorcing, how did you respond?

What were you feeling? Were you scared? Did you think it would last?

How did you find out? Did your parents tell you? What did they say?

What questions did you have? Do you still have them?

Do you ever wonder if, because this has happened to your parents, it might happen to you someday? If so, how does that make you feel?

Are there times when you are too embarrassed or sad to tell your friends that your parents are separated or divorced? What do you say? How can we help make this easier for you to do?

Will you go or grow through this experience? The choice is yours. What is a goal you have for the end of our weeks together?

Week 1

Taking It Home

Toward Others... Questions to take to others:

> Healing cannot become complete without affecting the lives of those around us. Be courageous and go outside your comfort zone to take a risk and work on your relationships with others. This is application time - time to take what you have learned and apply it to your own individual experience.

Does divorce run in your family? Who has been divorced? How does that make you feel?

Do you feel like you have some "unfinished business" with either or both of your parents? What is it? Make a plan to settle it.

If you have had a bad attitude at home lately, what can you do this week to get off the ride (that is, take the tensions down and relieve the stress)?

What do other people, especially your friends, think about your parents being separated or divorced? What have they said? How does that make you feel?

List all the people you know who also have parents who are divorced or separated.

Week 1

Taking It Home

Toward God... Questions to take to God:

> When you ask God a question, expect His Spirit to respond to your heart. Be careful not to rush it, or manufacture an answer. Don't jot down your idea of the "right answer." Just pose the question to God, and wait on Him to speak personally to your heart.

God only asks us to be willing to listen. What do you think He would say to you today if you had lunch together?

Do you honestly think that God is there for you, or do you feel you are all alone? Why do you feel that way?

If you were to describe who God is to you right now, what would you say? (A friend, an acquaintance, someone you try to ignore, someone you are mad at, a father figure, or someone you don't really know?)

Week 1

HELPING CHILDREN DEAL WITH

The Anger Mask

When dealing with an angry child, it is critical that you realize that anger often masks other emotions like:

- Anxiety
- Confusion
- Danger
- Depression
- Fear
- Grief
- Guilt
- Powerlessness
- Sadness
- Shame

Anger: A strong feeling of displeasure & belligerence aroused by a wrong; wrath; ire.
dictionary.com

Scripture References

- Ps. 4:4
- Ps. 30:4-5
- Ps. 37:8
- Ps. 145:8
- Prov. 14:9
- Prov. 15:1
- Prov. 16:32
- Prov. 17:27
- Prov. 18:31
- Prov. 29:11
- Ecc. 7:9
- Mt. 5:22
- Lk. 6:31
- Eph. 4:26-27
- Eph. 4:31-32
- Col. 3:8
- Jms. 1:19-20

The three keys to helping CHILDREN deal with anger are recognizing it, naming it and learning ways to cope with it. Help kids recognize the early signs of anger like tensing of the body, clenching of fists, restlessness, deep breathing and widening of the eyes. Help them to name their anger by recognizing it on a scale from irritated to enraged. Finally give kids an arsenal of things they can do on their own to deal with anger when they feel it coming on - things like deep breathing, physical activity, draw a picture or listen to music. The most important thing is to let them know it's ok to be angry but you have to deal with it appropriately.

What To Say/Do

- How can I help?
- Tell me about that.
- Tell me your point of view.
- What choices do you have?
- Would you like a 5 or 10 minute break?
- I care too much about you to argue.
- I'm here for you. I love you. You're safe.
- What has helped before?

What NOT To Say/Do

- Do not engage in a power struggle.
- Do not react out of your own emotions.
- Do not assume you know everything or why the child is angry.
- Do not try to "reason" with them or try to "make them understand."
- Do not ignore or deny their anger.
- Do not blame yourself or take it personally. Kids lash out at the people closest to them.

http://Hope4HurtingKids.com

© 2017

Step by Step

GOALS

This week we want to:
1. Begin building friendships
2. Learn about denial—"What Is Denial?"
3. Talk about bargaining—"What Does It Mean?"
4. Discuss depression—"What Can I Do When I Am Feeling Blue?"
5. Know your rights as a child of divorce
6. Review the "Taking It Home" assignments

SOMETHING TO THINK ABOUT

We hope you have met some new friends here. One of the best things about a group like this is that it can help you realize you are not alone. There are many others who are experiencing the same pain and disappointment that you are experiencing or have experienced. We hope you take this opportunity to reach out to others and share your experiences with us.

In this session, we will go through three of the six stages of grief: denial, bargaining, and depression. We want you to realize they are all part of the grieving process, and it is important to allow yourself to understand, accept, and embrace them.

Our prayer for you this week is that you will find the strength and courage to be open and honest about how you're doing in the grieving process.

**Lesson Two
Week 2**

Verses of the week:

"Be strong and take heart, all you who hope in the LORD."

Psalm 31:24

Be Blessed!

"May our Lord Jesus Christ himself and God our Father, who loved us and by his grace gave us eternal encouragement and good hope, encourage your hearts and strengthen you in every good deed and word."

2 Thessalonians 2:16–17

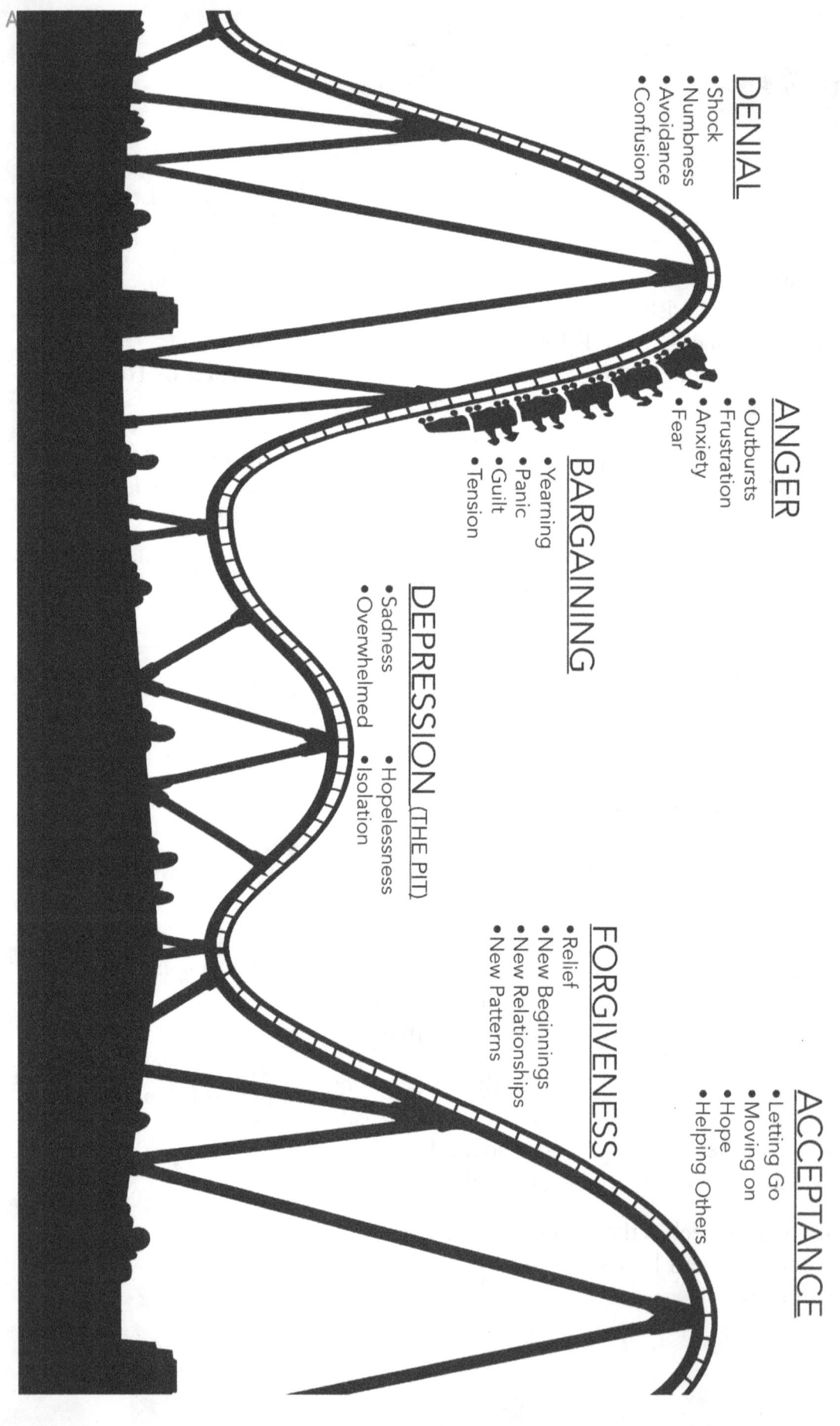

Denial ~ A negotiation in logic or a refusal to admit the truth or reality.

Denial is choosing to ignore our _____ feelings or circumstances and telling ourself _____ to help take away the pain.

Denial Says:

When my friends didn't invite me to their party… "That's okay, I didn't want to go anyway."

When no one asks me out for a date… "That's okay, because I don't have time to date right now."

Denial and Divorce

"It's okay that Mom and Dad got a divorce because it is more peaceful not having him/her around."

"So what if my parents got divorced? I'll just be living at home for a few more years. It won't effect me. I'll hardly even notice."

"I don't mind at all that Dad has left us; I can do whatever I want now."

The trauma and pain that goes along with separation and divorce is not over quickly. The loss is incomplete, and the pain is ongoing. Denial can be helpful in dealing with the shock of our emotions during traumatic experiences. But if we stay in a state of denial, it can become hurtful to us.

Don't get stuck in denial - tell the truth!

Be _____ with yourself. Don't try to cover your pain with denial or try to minimize what has happened. Chances are, you have been deeply hurt and you need to deal with that hurt. Denying an emotional problem does not make it go away.

Be _____ with God. God is not a god of denial. He wants us to be honest with ourselves, our emotions, and our circumstances and deal with them in His power. Jesus in His life proved that denial was not the way to tackle the tough, painful issues of life. In the Garden of Gethsemane, He realized He was going to face the worst possible pain imaginable at the cross. Jesus faced His painful emotions head-on.

Jesus Is Our Example

Matthew 26: 36-39

Then Jesus went with his disciples to a place called Gethsemane, and he said to them, "Sit here while I go over there and pray." He took Peter and the two sons of Zebedee along with him, and he began to be sorrowful and troubled. Then he said to them, "My soul is overwhelmed with sorrow to the point of death. Stay here and keep watch with me." Going a little farther, he fell with his face to the ground and prayed, "My Father, if it is possible, may this cup be taken from me. Yet not as I will, but as you will."

According to these verses, how did Jesus feel?
_____
_____
_____
_____

According to this passage, what did He do with His pain?
_____
_____
_____
_____

Jesus was in so much pain, He knew it was His time to die. In the midst of this fear, pain, and hurt, He did not deny it. He faced it head-on. He talked with the Father about the agony He would have to face on the cross, and He went to the cross to experience all of our sufferings and pain. He went face-to-face with the pain and hurt, and He did not back down. And just as Jesus faced His pain, you must face yours. Dealing with the truth about your parents' divorce will bring you face-to-face with awful pain. It will hurt, but it will be a step toward the truth. And it will lead you to freedom and healing, not denial and shame.

Bargaining ~To negotiate or bring to a desired level

Usually when we think of bargains, we think of sales or a good deal we found on our most recent shopping spree. But this kind of bargaining is a little different.

Bargaining and Divorce

When one of our parents leaves home, we usually want to do anything we can to bring them back together again. Unfortunately, it is not up to us and it is not within our power. Your parents did not separate or get a divorce because of anything you did or didn't do. It was a choice that they made. They did not separate because you forgot to make your bed one too many times, or because you fought with your brother or sister. It had nothing to do with you; it was a choice they made and there is nothing you can do to bring them back together. There is no "deal" you can make that will change their minds. It is their choice.

Negotiation

Another way to look at bargaining is trying to make a negotiation. "I'll do this for you, if you do that for me." Why do you think we do this? Do we really think we have the power to change the situations that surround us? Does God really make decisions based on the best offer?

Bargaining Says:

"God, if You help me get an A on this math test, I promise to study every night for an hour."

"Please don't let me get a ticket. I promise I will never speed again."

"I will never fight with my brother again, God, if You just bring Dad back home."

"I'll do better in school and help at home if you just bring Mom and Dad back together."

A Prayer for You to Pray

Lord, show me Your mercy and healing grace. I don't understand why this is happening to me, and I'm not sure how to resolve this crisis in my life. Help me to give up the need to be in control and to trust that You will show me the way. When I am tempted to strike a bargain with You or others, remind me of Your unconditional gift of love and forgiveness. Amen.

Questions for you to answer:

Have you ever made a bargain or tried to negotiate with God? If so, what was it about? Did it work?

How does God's unconditional gift of love fit into our attempts to bargain?

Depression ~ A state of feeling sad

What to do when you are feeling blue

Complete this worksheet as best you can. Put it in a place where you can refer to it whenever you start feeling depressed or anxious. During those particular times, pull it out and remind yourself what you can do. Sometimes when you are feeling too overwhelmed, it may be helpful to have some ideas in front of you in black and white. This may make it easier to take the actions necessary to work yourself out of the slump you are in.

My three favorite people to talk with are:
_____ Phone: _____
_____ Phone: _____
_____ Phone: _____

My favorite place to go is: _____
My favorite meditation/prayer is: _____
Music that makes me feel better is: _____
Books I'd like to read are: _____
_____

Movies I'd like to see are _____
_____

Puzzles or games I enjoy and can do are _____
_____

Physical activities I enjoy and can do are _____
_____

Ideas or plans to reorganize my room are _____
_____

My next goal is _____
_____

List the first three steps to accomplish this goal:
_____
_____
_____

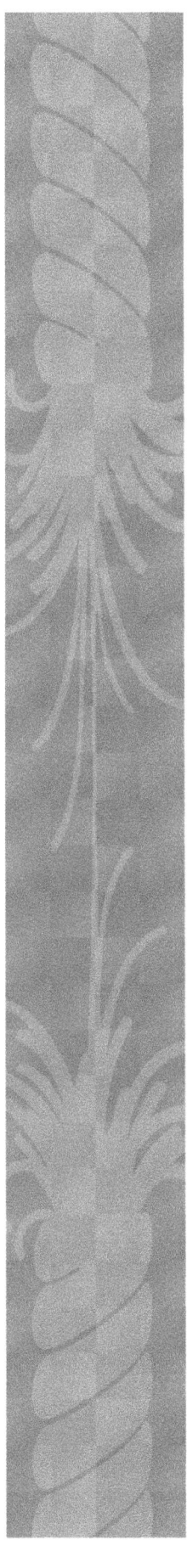

Children's Bill of Rights

Childrens Rights in Divorce Must Be Honored

1. The right to be treated as an interested and affected person and not as a pawn or possession

2. The right to love each parent, without feeling guilt, pressure, or rejection

3. The right to receive love, care, discipline, and protection from both parents

4. The right not to choose sides or be asked to decide where they want to live

5. The right to express their feelings about the divorce, such as anger, sadness, or fear

6. The right to a positive and constructive ongoing relationship with each parent

7. The right not to make adult decisions

8. The right to remain a child, without being asked to take on parental responsibilities or be an adult companion or friend to the parent

9. The right not to participate in the painful games parents play to hurt each other or be put in the middle of their battles

10. The right to the most adequate level of economic support that can be provided by the best efforts of both parents

The Journey: Divorce Through the Eyes of a Teen
www.sonsetpointministries.com

Taking It Home

Toward Yourself... Questions to take to my heart:

> Look into your heart as you answer these questions. This is introspection time — time to grapple with what drives your thinking and behavior. Be sure to "capture your thoughts."

Denial –

Did you experience denial when your parents split up?
____ Yes
____ No
____ I don't know
____ I think I'm still in denial
____ No way, not me, I'm fine

What did you deny? (Or what are you currently trying to deny?)
____ That your parents were/are divorcing
____ That this is/was just temporary
____ That one or both of your parents did something wrong
____ That you are/were depressed
____ That you are/were mad at either or both of your parents

Bargaining –

How have you tried bargaining?
____ I tried to get my parents back together
____ I tried to fix a problem
____ I promised God to be good if He would change things
____ I sabotaged a parent's new relationship
____ I haven't tried to bargain

Depression –

Are you feeling depressed right now?
____ No, I was, but I got over it
____ No, I haven't reached that point yet
____ No, I think I sailed right past it
____ Yes, it is very hard and lonely
____ Yes, I think I'm stuck in it
____ Yes, but I feel like I'm doing pretty good now

How long have you been feeling depressed?

Do you think this is something you should talk to someone about?

How is depression affecting your life? (Check all that apply)

____ Not sleeping well ____ Nothing is fun anymore
____ Not eating right ____ Lack of concentration
____ Sick a lot ____ School grades are suffering
____ Feeling like giving up ____ Sad all the time
____ Crying a lot ____ Preoccupation with death

Week 2

Taking It Home

Toward Others... Questions to take to others:

> Healing cannot become complete without affecting the lives of those around us. Be courageous and go outside your comfort zone to take a risk and work on your relationships with others. This is application time — time to take what you have learned and apply it to your own individual experience.

Do you ever blame yourself for your parent's separation/divorce? If so, why?

Have you ever tried to manipulate someone or a situation to get what you wanted?

    Did it work?

    How did it make you feel afterward?

Has something happened recently that you tried to pretend didn't happen? What was it?

Is anyone in your family denying the reality of the divorce? If so, how can you help?

How has being in any of these stages of grief affected other people in your life?

Have any of your relationships changed as a result of the divorce or separation? If so, how?

Week 2

Taking It Home

Toward God... Questions to take to God:

> When you ask God a question, expect His Spirit to respond to your heart. Be careful not to rush it, or manufacture an answer. Don't jot down your idea of the "right answer." Just pose the question to God, and wait on Him to speak personally to your heart.

Is it easier or harder to have hope right now? Why?

Have you ever made a promise to God as a way of bargaining? What was it?

Do you blame God for allowing this to happen to your family?

Ask God what negative thoughts and behaviors are holding you captive to your depression. Ask Him to help you decide what is reasonable depression, given what you're going through, and what is harmful depression that needs attention.

Set aside time to talk to God on a daily basis about whatever you wish. Try it every day for at least one week then consider the effect it has on you.

Week 2

Getting a Grip

Lesson Three
Week 3

GOALS

This week we want to:
1. Explore the effects of anger
2. Focus on "Getting a Grip" on your anger
3. Identify healthy ways to deal with anger
4. Learn better ways to resolve your conflicts
5. Recognize your "Anger Warning Signs"
6. Review the "Taking It Home" assignments

Verses of the week:

"My dear brothers and sisters, take note of this: Everyone should be quick to listen, slow to speak and slow to become angry, because human anger does not produce the righteousness that God desires."

James 1:19–20

Be Blessed!

"So use every piece of God's armor to resist the enemy whenever he attacks, and when it is all over, you will still be standing up."

Ephesians 6:13 (TLB)

SOMETHING TO THINK ABOUT

Anger is a tricky emotion. It attacks when we don't even realize it is there. In this session we are going to learn that not all anger is wrong; there are times when we can be justified in our anger. We need to focus on our intent when we are angry. Are we purposely trying to hurt someone? Are we acting out in order to get revenge? Or are we allowing our anger to control our thinking rather than allowing our thinking to control our anger?

Expressing your frustrations can be good if it is controlled and used as a way of setting healthy boundaries. How do you express your anger? In this session, you will discover healthy skills to help you cope with and control your anger.

Our prayer for you this session is that God will give you patience and compassion as you learn healthy ways to deal with and express your anger.

Your Anger Grip

Check the things you're likely to do when you're angry.

- ☐ Push or hit someone
- ☐ Hit or damage things
- ☐ Throw things
- ☐ Pick fights at home, at school or when playing sports
- ☐ Tease or mock others
- ☐ Yell or scream at those you're angry with
- ☐ Insult or threaten others
- ☐ Criticize others
- ☐ Act sick
- ☐ Blame someone else
- ☐ Kick or torment a pet
- ☐ Drive recklessly
- ☐ Slam doors
- ☐ Put holes in walls

- ☐ Talk yourself out of feeling angry
- ☐ Feel as if you're being bad or sinful if you get angry
- ☐ Feel that someone won't like or love you if you get angry
- ☐ Give in to avoid another's anger
- ☐ Laugh nervously instead of appearing angry
- ☐ Ignore whoever upsets you
- ☐ Get silent and moody
- ☐ Think that God might punish you for being angry
- ☐ Try to fix the situation
- ☐ Take the blame just to end the conflict
- ☐ Walk on eggshells everywhere
- ☐ Get a nervous stomach

How many checks do you have in the left column? _____
These are times when you are OVER REACTING.

How many checks do you have in the right column? _____
These are times when you are UNDER REACTING.

HOW DO I RESPOND TO CONFLICT?

Rate yourself on the following statements, 5 meaning you do it very well, and 1 meaning you need improvement.

1. Don't fight to win. Nobody wins when you do. Remember that you are trying to solve the problem, not win the fight. Be willing to negotiate or give in when necessary.

Rate yourself: I do this—
Very Well   Sometimes   Needs Improvement
5   4   3   2   1

2. Be sure that you understand exactly what the problem is. If you are not sure why you are having a conflict, discuss it with one another first.

Rate yourself: I do this—
Very Well   Sometimes   Needs Improvement
5   4   3   2   1

3. Take care of a problem when it comes up. Don't let it get too big to handle. Even if the problem seems small, if you don't deal with it at the time it happens, the problem will only get bigger. Don't let things stew.

Rate yourself: I do this—
Very Well   Sometimes   Needs Improvement
5   4   3   2   1

4. Talk about only one conflict at a time. Don't throw up all the old issues that have happened in the past. Stick to the problem that you are having at the moment.

Rate yourself: I do this–
Very Well		Sometimes		Needs Improvement
5	4	3	2	1

5. Don't blame others for problems you are having with someone else. If you are mad at your brother, don't yell at your best friend. Directly tell each person what is bothering you, and do not let it affect your other relationships.

Rate yourself: I do this–
Very Well		Sometimes		Needs Improvement
5	4	3	2	1

6. Think before you speak. If you say mean things to your family or friends or speak sarcastically to them even though you may just be teasing, you are really hurting them. If you have something constructive to say, be sure that you say it in a way that will be helpful and not harmful.

Rate yourself: I do this–
Very Well		Sometimes		Needs Improvement
5	4	3	2	1

7. Never strike another person to get your way. Physical violence or abuse (hitting, punching, kicking, or slapping) is NEVER acceptable behavior.

Rate yourself: I do this–
Very Well		Sometimes		Needs Improvement
5	4	3	2	1

8. Try writing down your feelings. If the person you are having a conflict with will not discuss the problem, or if you are not comfortable enough to talk with him or her about it, write a letter or e-mail. You can decide later whether you want to mail it or send it. Even though you aren't able to talk it over with the other person, you will understand more about how you feel when you read your words over again.

Rate yourself: I do this–

Very Well		Sometimes		Needs Improvement
5	4	3	2	1

9. Listen to what the other person has to say. Each person involved has his or her own point of view and should have the chance to express it. Learn to listen with both your mind and your ears.

Rate yourself: I do this–

Very Well		Sometimes		Needs Improvement
5	4	3	2	1

10. When the fight is over, drop it. Forgive and forget. Don't keep bringing up the fight or hold on to your anger once an argument is over, even if it was not resolved the way you wanted.

Rate yourself: I do this–

Very Well		Sometimes		Needs Improvement
5	4	3	2	1

MANAGING YOUR ANGER

Here are some safe and honest ways to release your angry feelings. You might not have a choice about becoming angry, but you do have a choice about how to cope with your feelings. Circle the ones that you would feel most comfortable doing.

1. Exercise.

2. Take a long, slow walk.

3. Cry.

4. Talk about it with someone you trust (a friend, parent, teacher, pastor, counselor, brother, sister, grandparent) who is a good listener.

5. Close your eyes, breathe deeply and let yourself feel angry until it slowly begins to fade away.

6. If you are very angry, don't watch violent movies or listen to really loud music. They may influence you and cause you to act in destructive ways.

7. Take a hot bath or a cold shower, whichever "cools" you down.

8. Work on any kind of puzzle or problem that needs solving. This will serve as a great distraction.

9. Listen to relaxing music.

10. Sing.

11. Write a letter or write in your journal.

12. Do anything that calms you down! Watch a sunset, gaze at the moon, sit by a lake.

13. Do anything you can think of that helps you to release your angry or tense feelings.

Try different ways of releasing your anger until you find one or two methods that work for you. After you have done something to calm yourself down and understand your feelings, make every effort to talk to the person with whom you are angry.

Anger Helps!

There are many things you can do to help yourself work through your anger. Here is a list of some suggestions you might consider. Check the items that you think might work for you.

- ☐ Talk to a friend you trust.
- ☐ Yell into a recorder, play it back, then erase it.
- ☐ Close your eyes and listen. Pay attention to the sounds that are farthest away, then those that are closest to you. Slowly stretch your arms and legs as you open your eyes.
- ☐ Breathe in slowly and deeply while counting to five, then breathe out slowly and deeply to another count of five.
- ☐ Find a quiet spot and shout at God about your feelings.
- ☐ Say nothing and just breathe and count to ten.
- ☐ Focus on something completely different.
- ☐ Smile; exercise those face muscles. It takes many more muscles to frown than it does to smile.
- ☐ Replace "hot thoughts" with "cool thoughts" by using positive self-talk. This means telling yourself messages like, "I can handle this. Stop and calm down. Stay in control."
- ☐ Tear up an old magazine or phone book. Rip each page out and crumple it up, then "throw away" your angry feelings by throwing the pages into the trash.
- ☐ Find a safe place to scream (or bury your face in a pillow and do so).
- ☐ Jog, exercise, or do some other physical activity.
- ☐ Hit a punching bag.
- ☐ Write about your angry feelings, or write a letter to the person with whom you are angry (but don't send it).

Make a promise to yourself to try at least two of the things you checked this week. If these help with your anger, great! If not, try something else next week ... and the next and the next. Since managing anger is a skill, it is important to find what works for you and to keep practicing it so that it becomes a strong resource for you.

Taking It Home
Toward Yourself... Questions to take to my heart:

> Look into your heart as you answer these questions. This is introspection time — time to grapple with what drives your thinking and behavior. Be sure to "capture your thoughts."

How would I rate my current level of anger?

1	2	3	4	5	6	7	8	9
cool		warm		simmering		very hot		boiling over

How would I rate my current effectiveness in handling my anger?

1	2	3	4	5	6	7	8	9
disastrous		ineffective		somewhat effective			very effective	

Which "Anger Helps" have you used this week and how have they worked?

What are some ways I am coping with my pain?

In what ways are my current coping skills helping me?

In what ways are my current coping skills hurting me?

What are the warning signs that signal me when I am getting angry? How can I plan to recognize when they are approaching, and defuse my anger?

Week 3

Taking It Home

Toward Others... Questions to take to others:

> Healing cannot become complete without affecting the lives of those around us. Be courageous and go outside your comfort zone to take a risk and work on your relationships with others. This is application time — time to take what you have learned and apply it to your own individual experience.

Are you angry at your parents right now? If so, why are you angry at them?

    I'm angry at my dad because:

    I'm angry at my mom because:

What would you like to say to either or both of your parents right now?

    Mom-

    Dad-

Take a minute to think about a recent time when you got angry. Did you over react? Did you direct it toward the right people? Or did you under react by holding it in? If you did express it, did you do it appropriately, or did you explode? If you under reacted, what were you afraid of?

Week 3

Taking It Home

Toward God... Questions to take to God:

> When you ask God a question, expect His Spirit to respond to your heart. Be careful not to rush it, or manufacture an answer. Don't jot down your idea of the "right answer." Just pose the question to God, and wait on Him to speak personally to your heart.

What questions about God does your family situation give you?

Do you feel that your anger could be out of control? Do you need Jesus to help you find ways to control it?

Do you believe anger is a sin? Why or why not?

Are you angry at God? If so, pray this prayer:

"God, it's not easy to admit that I am angry at You. What do You think of my anger toward You? What would You like to tell me about my anger? I know You know my every thought, so how do You feel about me right now?"

Week 3

Hurts Band-Aids Can't Cover

Lesson Four
Week 4

GOALS

This week we want to:
1. Evaluate your self-esteem
2. Look at "Who's to Blame?"
3. Recognize our "Anxiety Builders"
4. Identify the hurts you carry
5. Release your pain to God
6. Review the "Taking It Home" assignments

Verse of the week:

"Come to me, all you who are weary and burdened, and I will give you rest...."

Matthew 11:28

SOMETHING TO THINK ABOUT

The separation or divorce of your parents can cause you some very deep hurts. We understand that and want to help you work through those hurts. This week will not be easy as we learn to identify and embrace our pain, but it is a necessary part of the healing process.

Remember, this group is your "Safety Park." Nothing you say or share here will ever leave this room. It is very important for you not to rush through this process. Whatever hurts you are carrying will affect you in one way or another if they are left buried. The longer you hold unexpressed feelings inside, the deeper those feelings will go, and years later they may come back even stronger.

Please spend time searching deep within yourself to discover the hurts you have been holding on to. It is only by bringing them to the surface and dealing with them that you can move beyond the pain. Wouldn't you like to be free from the hurt, anger, and disappointment you have been experiencing?

Our prayer this week is for you to allow Jesus to carry your burdens so you may fully experience His peace and be able to rest in the comfort of His embrace.

Be Blessed!

"The LORD is a refuge for the oppressed, a stronghold in times of trouble. Those who know your name trust in you, for you, O LORD, have never forsaken anyone those who seek you."

Psalm 9:9–10

Self-Esteem Scale

On the scale below, mark each statement that relates to you.

_____ I feel I can reach my goals.

_____ I have a lot to be proud of.

_____ I can accept criticism without feeling put down.

_____ I feel valued and needed.

_____ I don't need other's approval to feel good.

_____ I feel happy and carefree.

_____ I can make friends easily.

_____ I know I am not a failure.

_____ I enjoy socializing.

_____ I pretty much accept myself.

_____ I have a number of good qualities.

_____ I deserve love and respect.

_____ I have a hard time making friends.

_____ I feel guilty about asking for what I need.

_____ I hide my true feelings.

_____ I feel less than others.

_____ I feel like a failure.

_____ I think the world would be better off without me in it.

Self-Esteem Check-Up

How's your self-esteem doing these days? Check it out!

After each statement in the first column, write an "A" if you agree or a "D" if you disagree. After you complete the first column, go to the next page and calculate your points.

	"A" or "D"	Points
1. I get along with most people most of the time.	_____	_____
2. I'm doing my best at school and it shows.	_____	_____
3. When people criticize me, I get angry and snap back.	_____	_____
4. I sometimes drink alcohol or do drugs when my friends pressure me, just to be accepted.	_____	_____
5. When I fight with my friends or siblings and get into trouble for it, I say it was their fault, even when it was mine.	_____	_____
6. It's easy for me to compliment others.	_____	_____
7. I'm pretty obedient and follow rules easily.	_____	_____
8. I often say, "I don't know" or "I don't care," even when I do.	_____	_____

After each statement in the first column, write an "A" if you agree or a "D" if you disagree. After you complete the first column, go to the next page and calculate your points.

	"A" or "D"	Points
9. I hate how I look.	_____	_____
10. My parents listen to me, and I feel my thoughts have value.	_____	_____
11. When God made me, He made something beautiful.	_____	_____
12. I have a good friend whom I can talk to about anything.	_____	_____
13. I make friends easily.	_____	_____
14. I'm pretty close to my mom and dad.	_____	_____
15. I feel safe with my mom and dad.	_____	_____
16. When I get mad, I swear a lot.	_____	_____

Self-Esteem Score Sheet

Now give yourself the following points for each statement and write them in the "Points" column on the previous pages.

1. Agree .... 2 points
   Disagree ... 1 point

2. Agree .... 2 points
   Disagree ... 1 point

3. Agree .... 1 point
   Disagree ... 2 points

4. Agree .... 1 point
   Disagree ... 2 points

5. Agree .... 1 point
   Disagree ... 2 points

6. Agree .... 2 points
   Disagree ... 1 point

7. Agree .... 2 points
   Disagree ... 1 point

8. Agree .... 1 point
   Disagree ... 2 points

9. Agree .... 1 point
   Disagree ... 2 points

10. Agree .... 2 points
    Disagree ... 1 point

11. Agree .... 2 points
    Disagree ... 1 point

12. Agree .... 2 points
    Disagree ... 1 point

13. Agree .... 2 points
    Disagree ... 1 point

14. Agree .... 2 points
    Disagree ... 1 point

15. Agree .... 2 points
    Disagree ... 1 point

16. Agree .... 1 point
    Disagree ... 2 points

Total Your Points:

22 points: You have very strong self-esteem. Good for you! Even in the midst of the changes, you are doing great.

20-21 points: You're on the right path. Keep up the good work! Even though things are rough right now, you are staying above the water.

18-19 points: There's a lot that's good about you, but you're not recognizing it. Find a good friend to boost your confidence.

16-17 points: You're feeling low and overwhelmed. You need to take action to help yourself. Find someone you can trust and talk with them.

BLAME GAME

How do you see it? When there is a problem, what is your first reaction?
Circle one letter for each question.

1. Your gut reaction to your parents' separation or divorce is:
   a. Maybe there is something I could have done (or could do) to change things.
   b. Mom and Dad are the ones who have to work out their problems. I'm staying out of it. Mom and Dad are responsible for themselves.
   c. I'm still angry, especially at my mom/dad. If he/she had been more responsible, my life would be okay.
   d. If God really loved me, He'd make my parents get back together (or make my parent be a better parent) and this wouldn't be happening to me.

2. Which of these statements best describes you?
   a. Succeeding in life is a lot like succeeding in school. You can achieve most anything you want, if you work at it.
   b. It's pretty easy for me to let go of a problem or situation I can't do anything about. You can control some things in life, but there's a lot you can't control, too. I understand that.
   c. There is always someone at fault in every problem. Those who are at fault are often the bad people.
   d. If I always try to be a good person, God will reward me with what I want.

3. Suppose two of your closest friends just had a really bad fight. How would you most likely respond to them?
   a. I would listen to what each has to say, then do my best to help them resolve their differences and mend the relationship.
   b. I would be supportive and listen to both of them. I wouldn't take sides, though, because I wouldn't want to lose either friend.
   c. I'd take the side of the friend whom I was closer to. That kind of loyalty is an important part of friendship.
   d. I'd take the side of the person who had better moral character.

4. When your friends come over for a party and they ask you where your other parent is, you respond by saying:

   a. Our family argued too much, so my mom/dad has moved out.
   b. My parents are having problems, so they have decided not to live together anymore.
   c. My mom/dad is a loser and left the family.
   d. Ever since my mom/dad left, God doesn't see us as a family anymore.

5. When your mom/dad doesn't come to your school concert or sporting event, you feel:

   a. If I was important and they loved me, they would be here.
   b. I know that they love me, but they are busy trying to keep things as normal as possible.
   c. If they don't care enough about me to come to my events, they won't care if I don't come home, either.
   d. Why did God give me such awful parents?

6. When you have to miss a party you were invited to, because you are with your other parent, you think:

   a. Why make friends when I won't be able to hang out with them anyway?
   d. It's important for me to be with my mom/dad. My friends will understand and I will try to invite them over to my house next weekend.
   c. This is not fair! Don't they care about my life? I can't wait until I don't have to listen to them anymore.
   d. God, why are You doing this to me? You know how important my friends are to me! How am I supposed to choose?

7. When my mom/dad doesn't come for a visitation, it makes me feel that:

   a. My mom/dad doesn't love me anymore. They must love their boyfriend/girlfriend more than me.
   b. I need to call my mom/dad or write them a letter and tell them how it made me feel.
   c. Forget it! I'm done! I'm not talking to him/her anymore.
   d. If she/he doesn't love me anymore, then God must not love me, either.

Which letter did you circle the most of?

As _____ Bs _____

Cs _____ Ds _____

BLAME GAME Results

Whom do you tend to blame when bad things happen?

IT'S ALL MY FAULT! If you circled mostly As, you're pretty hard on yourself. It's as if you're always frowning at yourself, telling yourself you should be doing more or feeling like you've screwed up. Blaming yourself when things go wrong is an appealing option, because it lets you believe that you have the power to fix things. The harder reality to face is that your parents have shortcomings and make mistakes, that their separation or divorce is not your fault, and that it is certainly beyond your fixing. While you have good intentions, you need to accept that you can't control other people's problems. It's time to start being good to yourself and give yourself a break. Don't give in to the false belief that you've caused any of this, because you have not. Stay out of your parents' conflict and let them handle it.

I'LL BE OKAY! If you circled mostly Bs, you are doing a good job of being fair, objective, and faithful to both of your parents. While it might not be easy, you avoid taking either parent's side, and you realize that only they can solve their problems. You recognize what you can and cannot control. You don't jump to conclusions, either. Instead, you try to get as many facts as possible before forming an opinion. Congratulations!

IT'S ALL YOUR FAULT! If you circled mostly Cs, your anger is controlling you. Maybe one parent has told you details about the separation or divorce that has turned you against the other. Or perhaps you've taken the side of the parent you feel you need to protect, or the one who treats you better. But a separation or divorce is never only one person's fault. Rarely is there just one "good guy" and one "bad guy." While one parent might seem to be more at fault than the other, both have some responsibility for the situation. Dumping all the blame on one parent isn't fair. It won't help you discover the truth; it won't help you feel any better. Taking anger out on your parents, or anyone else, is a destructive way of handling your feelings. While you may have good reason to be angry, the challenge is to find a constructive way to deal with those feelings. It starts with understanding your feelings and trying to forgive the parent with whom you're the most angry. This will help keep your anger from spilling over into all of your relationships and possibly jeopardizing friendships that could be supportive for you.

IT'S ALL GOD'S FAULT! If you circled mostly Ds, you're quick to blame God when things go wrong. You probably have a strong sense of right and wrong, which is good. You may get angry at God a lot, too, which is okay because God understands. The problem you run into is the common belief that God causes bad things to happen. When we're in the middle of something bad, we tend to ask, "Why me? Why did God let this happen?" Here's something very important to consider: God doesn't make bad things happen. Rather, God is a loving God, and out of love, He gives us free will. Because of this, everyone is free to make choices, which then could lead to mistakes. God doesn't promise anyone a problem-free life, no matter how good we are. What God offers, instead, is strength and direction to cope with our problems and grow from them.

Self-Esteem Worksheet

Rate from 0 to 10 how much you believe in each statement. "0" means you do not believe it at all, and "10" means you completely believe it.

_____ I believe in myself.
_____ I am just as valuable as other people.
_____ I would rather be me than someone else.
_____ I am proud of my accomplishments.
_____ I make friends easily.
_____ I think my parent's divorce is my fault.
_____ I feel good when I get a compliment.
_____ I can handle criticism.
_____ I am good at solving problems.
_____ I have a lot of friends.
_____ I am doing well in school.
_____ I am good at solving problems.

_____ I love trying new things.
_____ I respect myself.
_____ I am comfortable talking in front of others.
_____ I feel intimated often.
_____ I question my parent's love for me.
_____ I like the way I look.
_____ I love myself even when others reject me.
_____ I know my positive qualities.
_____ I think my parent's arguing is always about me.
_____ I would rather be home alone than with my friends.
_____ I focus on my successes and not my failures.
_____ I'm not afraid to make mistakes.
_____ I am happy to be me.

_____ Total Score

Overall, how would you rate your self-esteem on the following scale?

0 _____ 10

What would you need to change in order for you to move up one point on the rating scale? (For example, if you rated yourself a 6, what would need to happen for you to be at a 7?)

_____
_____
_____
_____
_____
_____
_____

De-Stress
in less than 10 minutes!

- Focus and notice your present surroundings.
- Do something nice for someone else.
- Look at a happy picture.
- Squeeze a stress ball.
- Walk, bike, or skateboard around the block.
- Read an inspirational quote.
- Watch a funny YouTube video.
- Visualize a safe and comforting place.
- Spend time with your pet.
- Write down ten things you are grateful for.
- Disconnect from tech.
- Practice deep, slow breathing.
- Practice yoga poses.
- Do 20 jumping jacks.
- Punch a pillow.
- Sit outside in the sun.
- Take a shower.
- Kick a ball around.
- Give yourself a neck massage.
- Listen to your favorite tunes.
- Head outside.
- Stretch.
- Meditate.
- Read a book.
- Count to ten.
- Dance.
- Journal.
- Doodle or draw.
- Tell some jokes.
- Call a friend.
- Chew a piece of gum.
- Pick some flowers.

Taking It Home

Toward Yourself... Questions to take to my heart:

> Look into your heart as you answer these questions. This is introspection time — time to grapple with what drives your thinking and behavior. Be sure to "capture your thoughts."

Has your parents' divorce stirred up any negative thoughts and feelings about yourself? If so, what are they? How do they affect your life?

Do you now or have you ever blamed yourself for your parent's divorce? Why? If you've worked through that, what helped you?

Set a goal for yourself. Make sure it is realistic, specific, and measurable with a deadline. For example: "I'm going to get a job and work at it for at least two months, so I can have money to go out with my friends."

Just because your life might be difficult now, that doesn't mean it always will be. Write about how you want your life to be in the future. For example, what career do you want to pursue? Will you marry and have children? Where do you want to live?

Week 4

Taking It Home
Toward Others... Questions to take to others:

> Healing cannot become complete without affecting the lives of those around us. Be courageous and go outside your comfort zone to take a risk and work on your relationships with others. This is application time — time to take what you have learned and apply it to your own individual experience.

What questions do you need to ask your parents that would relieve some unnecessary stress or worry in your life? When will you ask them?

Ask a close friend or family member what they like about you. Write down what they tell you.

Who is someone new you can bring into your life who will feed you with positive thoughts?

Who do you need to remove from your life because they fill you with too many negative thoughts?

Week 4

Taking It Home

Toward God... Questions to take to God:

> When you ask God a question, expect His Spirit to respond to your heart. Be careful not to rush it, or manufacture an answer. Don't jot down your idea of the "right answer." Just pose the question to God, and wait on Him to speak personally to your heart.

You are made in God's image. What does that mean to you? Read Genesis 1:27. Does God make mistakes?

What do you have to do to earn God's love and acceptance?

Imagine having a conversation with God. Ask how God sees you, then listen for God's voice in your heart. Write down what you hear God saying.

What does it mean to be "fearfully and wonderfully made"? Read Psalm 139:14.

Week 4

HELPING CHILDREN DEAL WITH STRESS

Signs of Stress in Kids

- Crying
- Problems Sleeping
- Aggression
- Nightmares
- Clinginess
- Moodiness
- Depression
- Fussiness
- Weight Issues
- Developmental Delays
- Regression
- Changing in eating habits
- Withdrawal

Stress: Constraining force or influence…that causes bodily or mental tension
Merriam-webster.com

Ps. 34:10	Mt. 11:28-30
Ps. 37:5	Jn. 14:27
Ps. 37:25	Jn. 16:33
Ps. 55:2	Rom. 8:6
Ps. 103:1-5	Rom. 8:37
Ps. 16:3	Rom. 16:20
Is. 40:28-31	1 Cor. 3:11
Is. 55:1-3	Gal. 6:9
Jer. 17:7	Ph. 4:6-9
Jer. 29:11	Heb. 3:17-19
Mal. 4:2	1 Pt. 5:6-7
Mt. 6:25-24	I Jn. 4:4

Scripture References

STRESS…SO MUCH FOR THE INNOCENCE OF YOUTH! The world of children today is marked by stress. Kids today face all kinds of stressors like school issues, bullying, family changes, death, divorce, health issues, "keeping up," social media, economic uncertainty being overextended, living up to parental expectations, peer pressure and more. Studies have shown that the effects of childhood stress are multiplicative so two stressor don't mean double the stress, but can mean much more stress in a child's life. This stress can lead to physical ailments, poor academic performance and, in some cases, suicide and often lasts well into adulthood.

What To Say/Do

- Lighten the mood.
- Stay calm
- "It's ok not to be perfect."
- Focus on the positives.
- "How can I help you?"
- "I know this is hard."
- "Tell me about it."
- "Help me move this wall." (Get them involved in physical activity.)
- Laughter.

What NOT To Say/Do

- "You're going to make yourself crazy."
- "What's wrong with you?"
- "You need to snap out of it."
- "Stressing out isn't going to make it better."
- "I can do it for you instead."
- "Practice makes perfect."
- "You'll be fine."
- "You have no reason to be stressed."
- "Trust me, it's all going to be ok."

http://Hope4HurtingKids.com

© 2017

Who Am I?

GOALS

This week we want to:
1. Better understand who you are
2. Work on bridging the past with the present
3. Discover Jesus in the midst of your pain
4. Understand your identity in Christ
5. Discuss the importance of taking good care of yourself
6. Review the "Taking It Home" assignments

SOMETHING TO THINK ABOUT

Sometimes when life turns upside down, you lose a sense of who you are. Circumstances and surroundings change, and you forget what life used to be like. In those times, you can lose a grip on who you really are. That's why we are going to celebrate "you" this week. We will bridge the gap between who you were before the separation or divorce and who you are today.

We are also going to share the love of Jesus with you. In this session, you will have an opportunity to receive Christ as your Savior and allow Him to help define who you are. With Christ in us, nothing is impossible. Our prayer is that you would receive Him today.

**Lesson Five
Week 5**

Verses of the week:

"And have put on the new self, which is being renewed in knowledge in the image of its Creator."

Colossians 3:10

Be Blessed!

"I praise you because I am fearfully and wonderfully made; your works are wonderful, I know that full well."

Psalm 139:14

Old Versus New

List below some things about you that have changed as a result of your parents' separation or divorce. For instance maybe you played basketball before the divorce, but you had to quit because of money or having to take care of your siblings after school. Maybe you used to be outgoing and now you just want to be alone. Or possibly you used to laugh all the time and now you are sad, or nothing used to bother you and now you are always angry. All of these things are situational, and hopefully after things settle down, you will be able to "be you" again. See how many of these changes you can come up with.

My Identity in Christ Scripture Find
Match the statements with the correct scripture passage.

___ Romans 8:15   A. Washed Clean

___ Isaiah 8:1   B. Light of the World

___ Galatians 5:1   C. Child of God

___ Deuteronomy 31:8   D. Never Alone

___ 2 Corinthians 3:12   E. Adopted into God's Family

___ 2 Corinthians 2:15   F. Heir of Christ

___ Galatians 3:26-29   G. Salt of the Earth

___ Matthew 5:13   H. Righteous

___ Matthew 5:14   I. God's Temple

___ John 15:15   J. Sweet Aroma

___ 1 Corinthians 3:16   K. Temple of the Holy Spirit

___ 1 Corinthians 3:9   L. God's Coworker

___ 1 John 3:1   M. Free

___ John 15:16   N. Branch of the True Vine

___ Jeremiah 31:3   O. Appointed to Bear Fruit

___ Zephaniah 3:17   P. Beloved

___ 1 Corinthians 6:19   Q. Bold

___ 2 Corinthians 5:21   R. Delighted In

✝ Who you are in Christ

Because you are in Christ, EVERY ONE of these statements is true for you.

I am Loved.
John 3:3

I am a joint heir with Jesus, sharing His inheritance with Him.
Romans 8:17

I am accepted.
Ephesians 1:6

I am Jesus' friend.
John 15:14

I am united with God and am one spirit with Him.
1 Corinthians 6:17

God works in me to help me do the things He wants me to do.
Philippians 2:13

I am seated in heavenly places with Christ.
Ephesians 2:6

I am a member of Christ's body.
1 Corinthians 12:27

I am redeemed and forgiven.
Colossians 3:14

I am a temple of God. His Spirit and His life lives in me.
1 Corinthians 6:19

I am a child of God.
John 1:12

I have been given exceedingly great and precious promises by God by which I share His nature.
2 Peter 1:4

I do not have the spirit of fear, but of love, power, and a sound mind.
2 Timothy 1:7

I am a saint.
Ephesians 1:1

I am complete in Jesus Christ.
Colossians 2:10

I can always know the presence of God because He never leaves me.
Hebrews 13:5

I am chosen to bear fruit.
John 15:16

I am a new creation because I am in Christ.
2 Corinthians 5:17

I have direct access to God.
Ephesians 2:18

I am God's coworker.
2 Corinthians 6:1

I am one of God's living stones, being built up in Christ as a spiritual house.
1 Peter 2:5

I am established, anointed, and sealed by God.
2 Corinthians 1:21

I am free from condemnation.
Romans 8:1

I am chosen of God, holy and dearly loved.
Colossians 3:12

I can ask God for wisdom, and He will give me what I need.
James 1:5

Self-Care Checklist

Negative Care

____ Overspend, overeat, and overindulge
____ Expect others to read your mind and meet your needs
____ Withhold success from yourself
____ Ignore your deepest desires but seek to fulfill the desires of others
____ Ignore your real emotions and put on a "happy" face
____ Push yourself beyond reasonable limits
____ Allow others to emotionally or physically take advantage of you
____ Deflect compliments
____ Say "yes" because you can't say "no"
____ Avoid time alone
____ Over exhaust yourself because of your need to feel important, needed, or worthy
____ Fear emotional intimacy
____ Try to do it all yourself, never asking for help
____ Try to appear perfect
____ Keep yourself so busy that you ignore your own needs
____ Accept blame for other people's actions
____ Either sleep too much or not enough

Positive Care

____ Take time for yourself
____ Allow yourself to make mistakes
____ Be open about your weaknesses
____ Reach out for help when needed
____ Spend time with friends
____ Rest
____ Play
____ Exercise
____ Eat well
____ Spend money wisely
____ Pursue your dreams
____ Share honestly with others
____ Make time to enjoy life with those you love
____ Forgive
____ Allow others to be disappointed in you without carrying shame
____ Appropriately express emotions, including anger and sadness
____ Tell others what they mean to you
____ Receive love from others
____ Say "yes" or "no" without guilt regarding either
____ Create a powerful support system
____ Celebrate accomplishments big and small
____ Smile and laugh often
____ Do things you enjoy
____ Find a hobby and do it regularly
____ Set healthy boundaries

Taking It Home

Towards Yourself... Questions to take to my heart:

> Look into your heart as you answer these questions. This is introspection time — time to grapple with what drives your thinking and behavior. Be sure to "capture your thoughts."

Were there any things you thought of but were afraid to put on or in your "Jesus bag"? What were they? Why were you afraid to share them?

What things in your bag are you proud of? Not proud of?

After doing your "Jesus bags" and seeing other's, what things would you like to improve about yourself?

Do you miss the "old you"? What are some things you can do to bring out that person again?

Week 5

Taking It Home

Toward Others... Questions to take to others:

> Healing cannot become complete without affecting the lives of those around us. Be courageous and go outside your comfort zone to take a risk and work on your relationships with others. This is application time — time to take what you have learned and apply it to your own individual experience.

Are your frustrations and hurts about your current home situation affecting those around you? Your relationships? Your grades? In what way?

What items did you pick for the "pick two" exercise and why?

Ask someone you trust what changes they have seen in you since your parents separated. Do you think these are good changes or bad changes?

Take your "Jesus bag" home and share it with one or both of your parents.

Week 5

Taking It Home

Toward God... Questions to take to God:

> When you ask God a question, expect His Spirit to respond to your heart. Be careful not to rush it, or manufacture an answer. Don't jot down your idea of the "right answer." Just pose the question to God, and wait on Him to speak personally to your heart.

If you have not previously asked Jesus into your heart, go to your leader, a pastor, or another Christian friend and do it right away! (See "Steps to Peace with God.")

If you asked Jesus into your heart during the group today, tell someone about it. Who did you tell, and how did they respond?

If you are not ready to receive Jesus into your life yet, ask Jesus to show Himself and His love to you this week.

Is the topic this week a whole new concept to you? If it is and you still have questions, write them down here and ask someone about them soon.

Week 5

Where Is God When It Hurts?

Lesson Six
Week 6

GOALS

This week we want to:
1. Learn more about God and His desire to comfort you
2. Read the story of Job in the Bible and compare it to your life
3. Build a support system around you
4. Consider "Letting It Go"
5. Allow God to comfort you
6. Review the "Taking It Home" assignments

Verses of the week:

"Be strong and courageous. Do not be afraid or terrified because of them, for the LORD your God goes with you; he will never leave you nor forsake you."

Deuteronomy 31:6

SOMETHING TO THINK ABOUT

Whom do you go to for comfort? Have they ever disappointed you? Have they ever let you down? Humans will fail us, but God promises never to let us down. Jesus has felt the same rejection, fears, mistrust, abandonment, loneliness, and insecurities as you have. He went from being happy and content, to complete rejection and loneliness. He felt the world come crashing in on Him, and those He trusted most did not stand by Him, either. Where did He go when He felt scared and all alone? He turned to God—His heavenly Father. Don't you think that if it worked for Him, it can work for us, too? God is reaching out to you—receive His comfort today.

Be Blessed!

"Because he loves me," says the LORD, "I will rescue him; I will protect him, for he acknowledges my name. He will call on me, and I will answer him; I will be with him in trouble, I will deliver him and honor him. With long life I will satisfy him and show him my salvation."

Psalm 91:14–16

The Story of Job

Long ago there was a man named Job who loved God very much. Job was a wise man, and had thousands of sheep and camels, and hundreds of oxen and donkeys. He also had seven sons and three daughters.

One day when the angels were standing before God, Satan came and stood with them. Satan told God, "Job loves you because You are so good to him. If Job were to lose everything he has, then he would turn away from You."

Later, Job lost all of his animals and all of his children. Job also became very sick with horrible sores all over his body. Job's wife because angry with God and tried to get Job mad at God. But Job did not. He still loved God.

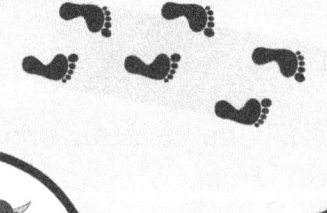

When Job's friends heard about what had happened, they came to visit him. They thought that maybe God was punishing him. They said, "You have lost everything, and you are covered with sores. Surely you have done something wrong, and God is punishing you."

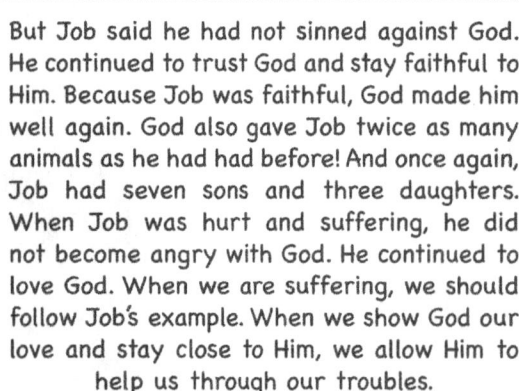

But Job said he had not sinned against God. He continued to trust God and stay faithful to Him. Because Job was faithful, God made him well again. God also gave Job twice as many animals as he had had before! And once again, Job had seven sons and three daughters. When Job was hurt and suffering, he did not become angry with God. He continued to love God. When we are suffering, we should follow Job's example. When we show God our love and stay close to Him, we allow Him to help us through our troubles.

Modern Day Job

1. What makes a "good" person?

2. Describe someone you know who is good.

3. How do you identify yourself good or bad?

4. How do your parents, teachers, and friends identify you?

5. Would God play with someone's life?

6. Why do you think this story is in the Bible?

7. What does it teach us about God? About life?

8. What kind of comfort did Job's friends offer him?

9. Would you want them as friends? Why or why not?

10. Describe the perfect friend. Do you have a friend like that? Are you a friend like your description?

11. Would any of Job's friends fit the description of a perfect friend? Why or why not?

12. If you had been Job's friend, what would you have done to help him?

13. After reading about Job's friends, what do you learn about offering advice?

14. What if you like your friends a lot but they recommend that you do something you know is bad? What would you do?

15. How do you stand up to your friends when they ask you to do something wrong?

16. What did God say to Job?

17. How would you have responded to God?

18. When did you last talk to God?

19. How often do you pray?

20. Why is it important to talk with God?

21. Would you argue with God or would you listen?

My LEGO Support System

Each of the blocks below have a spot for you to fill in the name of someone in your life who fits each category the best. Write down the name of one person in each box and see who your support system really is!

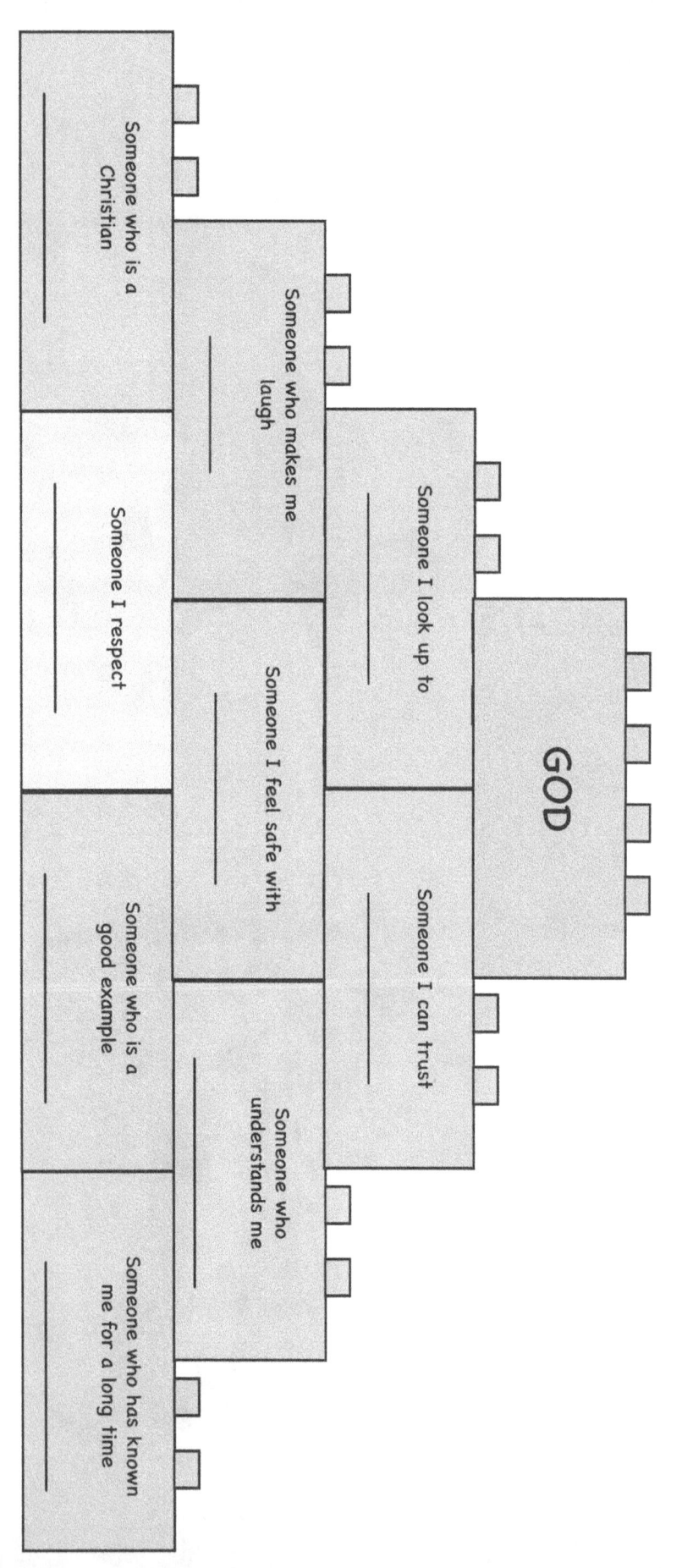

- Someone who is a Christian
- Someone who makes me laugh
- Someone I look up to
- GOD
- Someone I respect
- Someone I feel safe with
- Someone I can trust
- Someone who is a good example
- Someone who understands me
- Someone who has known me for a long time

Let It Go!

Not letting go will keep your spiritual life FROZEN

Read: Luke 9:57-62
1. **Letting Go of the Past**
   Philippians 3:13-14; Acts 8:3; Acts 9:1
2. **Letting Go of Relationships**
   Proverbs 4:14-15; 2 Corinthians 6:14-15
3. **Letting Go of Anxieties**
   1 Peter 5:7; Psalm 55:22
4. **Letting Go of Bitterness**
   Ephesians 4:31-32
5. **Letting Go of the Flesh**
   2 Corinthians 5:15-17; Galatians 2:20

What do you think holds you back from letting go?

Do you need to let go of any of these?

Anger	Hurt Feelings
Anxieties (Worry)	Lying Tongue
Bad Attitude	Materialism
Bad Habits	Mean Spirit
Bad Mood	Negativity
Bitterness	Pride
Control	Resentment
Disappointment	Selfishness
Fear	The Past
Foul Mouth	Unconfessed Sin
Frustration	Unforgiving Heart
Gossip	Unhealthy Relationships
Grumpiness	Wasting Time
Guilt	Worldly Influences

What do you want to let go of in order to move forward in your walk with the Lord?

Write down today's date to remind you of this decision to let go.
I am letting go.
_____
(date)

Letting Go...
Allows God to Move
Allows God to Heal
Allows Your Faith to Grow
Allows You to Move Forward

Jesus said, "No procrastination. No looking back. You can't put God's kingdom off till tomorrow. Seize the day."
~See Luke 9:62

Taking It Home

Toward Yourself... Questions to take to my heart:

> Look into your heart as you answer these questions. This is introspection time — time to grapple with what drives your thinking and behavior. Be sure to "capture your thoughts."

What part of a "Father's Love Letter" impacted you the most? What can you do to remind yourself of these promises?

It is important to take care of yourself. List three self care items you intend to work on this week.

It hurts when people we love and trust disappoint us. How do you deal with those disappointments?

Call someone in your Lego Support System. Whom did you call and why? Were they able to help you this week?

Week 6

Taking It Home

Toward Others... Questions to take to others:

> Healing cannot become complete without affecting the lives of those around us. Be courageous and go outside your comfort zone to take a risk and work on your relationships with others. This is application time — time to take what you have learned and apply it to your own individual experience.

What are some things God is telling you to let go of from others so that you can move on? What is your plan to do this?

Have you ever had friends or family members accuse you of doing or saying anything that has caused issues in your family?

If you were to take one of your siblings aside and tell them something you have learned in these lessons so far, who would you pick and what would you say? Now, can you actually do it?

How do you handle it when your parents disappoint you? Can you talk to them about how the disappointment made you feel? Can you still trust them?

Week 6

Taking It Home

Toward God... Questions to take to God:

> When you ask God a question, expect His Spirit to respond to your heart. Be careful not to rush it, or manufacture an answer. Don't jot down your idea of the "right answer." Just pose the question to God, and wait on Him to speak personally to your heart.

Do you think your parents' separation or divorce is moving you closer or farther away from God? Circle a number on the scale from 1 to 10 to indicate where you stand in relation to God these days.

1   2   3   4   5   6   7   8   9   10

Would you say that your feelings about God right now are mostly positive, mostly negative, or confusing?

Deep down, do you feel as if God has let you down? Tell God exactly why you feel that way. And then listen to what He says through the Bible, through a pastor or a youth leader, or through that quiet voice inside you... Chances are, He's saying something like, "Here, let Me help you. I know it is hard. I'll explain later, just trust Me." What do you think He is saying to you?

What do you think the phrase "Bad things happen to good people" means? Read 1 Corinthians 10:13 and explain how it relates to this saying.

Have you ever felt like Job's friends: perhaps thinking this divorce is a punishment from God for something you did or did not do? After reading Job's story, do you still feel the same way? What part of Job's story could you relate to the most?

Week 6

Feelings Tune-up

GOALS

This week we want to:
1. Identify your feelings
2. Understand healthy and unhealthy feelings
3. Recognize and prevent being "Caught in the Middle"
4. Learn better ways to process your feelings
5. Discover the need for setting personal boundaries for yourself and your grieving process
6. Complete the "Good Choice versus Bad Choice" exercise and discover the natural consequences of our choices
7. Review the "Taking It Home" assignments

Note: This chapter addresses ways to deal with ongoing conflict that may exist between your parents. If you have a parent who is uninvolved, or no longer living, you may want to consider some other relationships that currently cause conflicts for you.

SOMETHING TO THINK ABOUT

Feelings can be rough. Good–Bad, Big–Small, Happy–Sad, Easy–Tough, Shallow–Deep. They come in all shapes and sizes. During a separation or divorce, many, many feelings emerge—so many that you probably don't know what to do with them all. We're going to work together on recognizing them and learning how to express them in healthy ways. One of the toughest situations our parents can put us in is being stuck in the middle between them and their conflict. Maybe it's in the form of being a messenger, or an informant, or just a sounding board. Being put in this position is very difficult. We want to give you the tools necessary to help when you get put in situations like this.

We will also help you recognize the warning signs when this is happening, and help you set healthy boundaries to protect yourself from getting routinely stuck. Remember, you have every right to love and respect both of your parents. Our goal is to discover the best ways to make that happen.

Note: If your situation involves your safety, it is very important that you seek additional help in setting appropriate boundaries. Your safety needs to come first. If you have concerns about this, please share them with your leaders.

**Lesson Seven
Week 7**

Verse of the week:

"I will go before you and level the mountains; I will break down gates of bronze and cut through the bars of iron. I will give you hidden treasures, riches stored in secret places, so that you may know that I am the LORD, *the God of Israel, who summons you by name."*

Isaiah 45:2–3

Be Blessed!

"You are my hiding place; you will protect me from trouble and surround me with songs of deliverance."

Psalm 32:7

Emotional Eruption

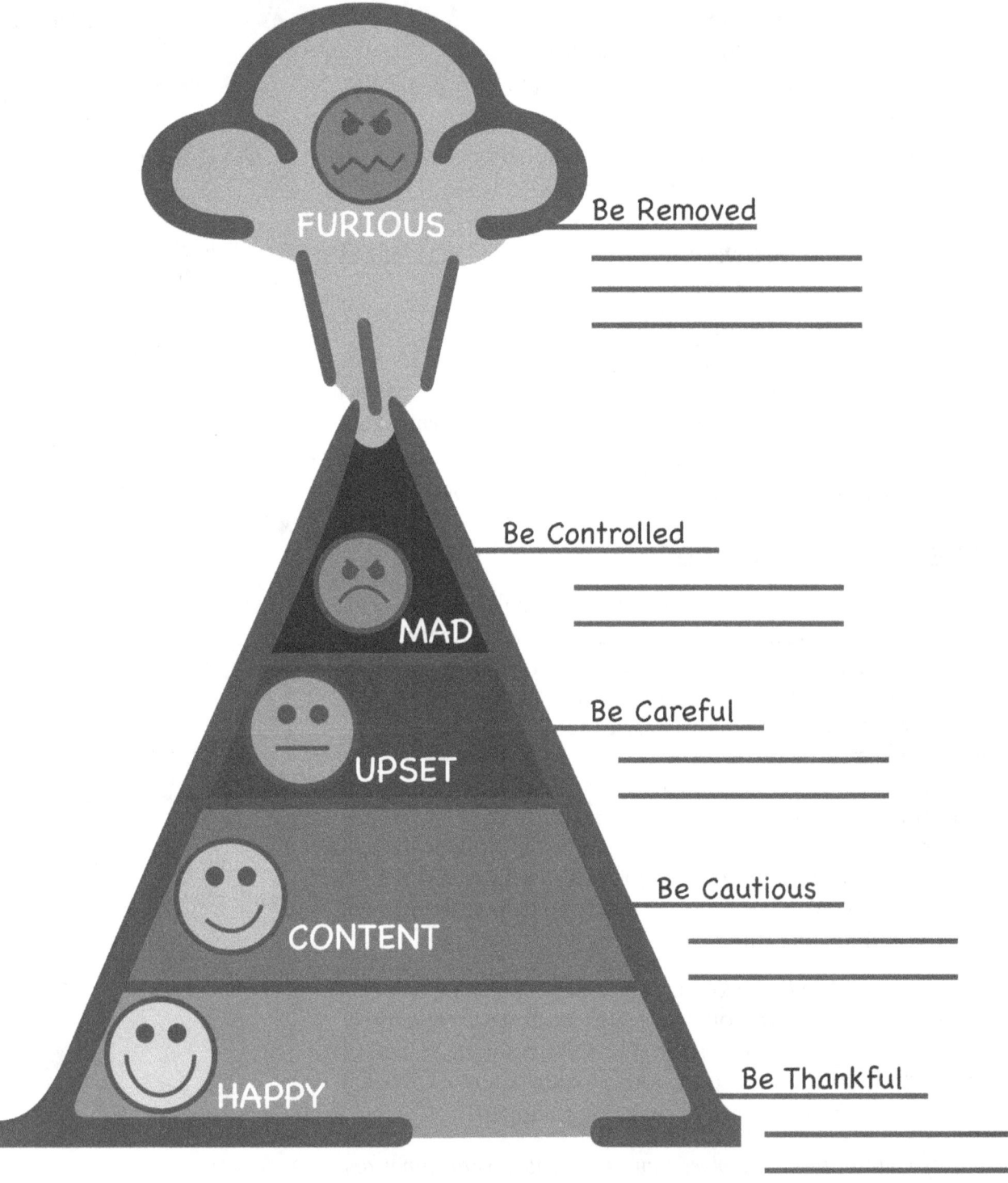

Getting a Grip

Check any of the things that you usually do when you're feeling down or depressed. Then go over your list and indicate whether they are healthy or unhealthy behaviors.

- ○ Watch a lot of TV
- ○ Take a walk
- ○ Talk to your best friend
- ○ Work out
- ○ Play video games
- ○ Drive recklessly
- ○ Mope around
- ○ Yell, pick a fight, or throw a tantrum
- ○ Talk to your pastor
- ○ Express your feelings creatively (for example, by drawing or playing an instrument)
- ○ Sleep too much or don't get out of bed
- ○ Talk to a pet
- ○ Think about ways you can physically hurt yourself
- ○ Cry
- ○ Pig out
- ○ Talk with God
- ○ Hurt yourself
- ○ Engage in sexual activity
- ○ Journal about how you feel
- ○ Purposely plan activities to stay away from home
- ○ Talk to a grandparent
- ○ Work hard at something (for example, by trying to get good grades or doing really well in sports)
- ○ Gamble
- ○ Talk with someone about how you're feeling (either in person or on the phone)
- ○ Use drugs, drink alcohol, or smoke cigarettes
- ○ Talk to a parent
- ○ Lock yourself in your room
- ○ Skip meals
- ○ Consider suicide
- ○ Bully others

ENTERING THE BATTLE FIELD

For each example below, circle the letter of the response that best reflects your actions:

When my parents put me in the middle of their arguing, I:
  a. Get so angry that we have a shouting match.
  b. Am never sure who's really right, so I side with the parent who's having a tougher time with the breakup.
  c. Try to avoid the situation.
  d. Tell them they're being unfair and to leave me out of it.

When I'm put in the battlefield, I often think that:
  a. My parents are completely clueless.
  b. I must be getting punished for doing something wrong.
  c. I should just ignore it.
  d. I shouldn't take it personally. This often happens when parents break up. This situation is tough for everyone.

The best way to handle the battlefield is to:
  a. Be as aggressive as I can. It's the best way to prevent the situation from getting worse.
  b. Try to please the parent I'm with. If I can get my parent in a better mood, maybe he or she will stop putting me in the middle.
  c. Try to escape by going to my room or a friend's house. Escaping by watching TV or listening to music helps, too.
  d. Try to stay objective, then confront the parent who's putting me in the battlefield as respectfully as I can.

When I am asked to deliver messages between my parents, I:
  a. Deliver the message.
  b. Don't say anything and ignore the situation.
  c. Say something completely different or incomplete.
  d. Remind my parent that I am not the mailman and that they need to take care of it themselves.

When I'm with one parent and my other parent calls and tries to convince me to do something else with them, I feel:
  a. Confused and torn, so I hang up the phone and go to my room to be alone.
  b. Angry at both parents for getting divorced and putting me in a position to have to choose.
  c. Confused, but I understand that although I want to be at both places, I can have fun wherever I am and with whomever.
  d. No pressure, because I understand that each parent has their time with me and another time will be available soon.

At Christmas or during any holiday, when I have to leave one home and go to the other parent's home, I respond by:
  a. Moping and pouting and not allowing anyone to enjoy themselves.
  b. Spending my holidays trying to make it easier for everybody else.
  c. Going back and forth, not connecting with anyone, afraid of getting close or having fun.
  d. Planning the day ahead of time, making the best of whatever time I have with both of my parents.

When I need shoes and one parent tells me to ask the other parent to buy them for me, I want to say:
  a. "Forget it! It's not worth it! I'll wear last year's shoes."
  b. "That's okay, I'll save my own money and buy them myself."
  c. "I'll borrow someone else's for a while until things calm down."
  d. "That's your issue with Mom/Dad. All I'm saying is that my shoes are too small and I need another pair. You guys figure out who's going to pay for them."

Every time one parent complains about child support, I want to:
  a. Scream.
  b. Talk to my parent and tell them this does not involve me and that I would wish it wouldn't be brought up again.
  c. Walk into my room and cry.
  d. Offer my parent some of my own money to help out.

Now, count up the number of times you circled each letter and note it below. This will give you a pretty good idea of how you handle the battlefield. Check out where you stand on the next page.

As _____   Bs _____

Cs _____   Ds _____

Which Animal Best Describes You on the Battlefield?

THE LION: If you circled mostly As, the battlefield gets you so angry that you negatively react and take it out on your parents, siblings, or friends. You might even take sides and join in your parents' anger. While it's normal to feel angry, dumping it on others never solves anything. When you react this way, it may help you feel in control, but it actually pushes people away.

It's time to stop using others as your punching bag. You need to explore constructive ways to get out your anger, so that you'll be able to work toward a solution. Talk to someone who can help you come up with alternative ways to express your frustration.

THE KITTY: If you circled mostly Bs, you tend to put others' feelings first while ignoring your own needs. Maybe you feel guilty about how you feel, or you fear getting punished if you speak your mind. Or perhaps you can't stand seeing your parents hurting, so you cover up your own feelings and try to cheer them up instead or play the peacemaker. You might even be blaming yourself, thinking, "I could have prevented all of this if I were a better kid."

While you have good intentions, you need to stick up for yourself and realize that it's your parents' job, not yours, to settle their problems. Their arguments are theirs. You are not responsible for their actions or to fix them. You also need to find a safe place where you can express your feelings and be heard; otherwise, your bottled-up feelings can snowball into bigger problems. Finally, reassure yourself that you have a right to love both your parents.

THE SNAKE: If you circled mostly Cs, you try to avoid conflict at all costs. Perhaps you think that the problem will magically go away, or maybe you've tricked yourself into thinking that someone else will solve it for you. In the meantime, you stay away from the house as much as possible to avoid your parents.

It's time to face the fact that there's no easy way out. Avoiding your parents will not solve anything. Instead, it can lead to worse problems. There are many things you can do to help yourself, such as talk straight to your parents about the problem. Or you might find it helpful to journal or draw your feelings about the battlefield, so you can understand more about what makes it stressful for you. Talking with a school counselor or another trusted adult can be helpful as well. It is always better to face your issues rather than run away from them. Usually they don't go away on their own; they just get worse.

THE PUPPY: If you circled mostly Ds, you do a good job of evaluating the battlefield with fairness and self-control. You don't let your emotions rule you. You stay in touch with who you are and what you want, which also serves you well. And when you stick up for yourself, you do so openly and respectfully — always the best approach for solving conflicts. Congratulations!

STUCK IN THE MIDDLE

How do your parents typically put you in the battlefield? Circle all the answers that apply. Then check whether your mom, your dad, or both of them do it.

WHAT MY PARENTS DO (OR DID)	WHO DOES (OR DID) IT?		
1. Ask me to be a messenger and/or spy.	Mom	Dad	Both
2. Bad-mouth the other.	Mom	Dad	Both
3. Scream or curse at the other in front of me.	Mom	Dad	Both
4. Force me to choose one parent over the other.	Mom	Dad	Both
5. Use guilt trips and/or threats.	Mom	Dad	Both
6. Put me down.	Mom	Dad	Both
7. Act more needy than the other parent, or ask for too much help or comfort.	Mom	Dad	Both
8. Buy me gifts or take me places in order to coax me to side against the other parent.	Mom	Dad	Both
9. Try to convince me not to want to be with the other parent.	Mom	Dad	Both
10. Say bad things about my other parent's significant other or new stepparent.	Mom	Dad	Both
11. Treat me like the informant on my other parent's life by asking who they are dating, where they are going, etc.	Mom	Dad	Both
12. Forget to pay for things to try to make the other parent pay.	Mom	Dad	Both
13. Transfer all of their hurt and pain onto my shoulders.	Mom	Dad	Both
14. Leave me at home night after night to babysit my siblings.	Mom	Dad	Both

BOOT CAMP!
What do you do to protect yourself?
Think about a time when your parents put you in the battlefield.
Write down how you felt and how you responded.

_____
_____
_____

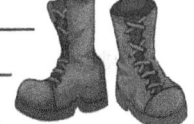

HOW TO STAY OFF THE BATTLEFIELD

Respond initially with silence; then share your thoughts with your parent respectfully.
When one parent bad-mouths the other, stay quiet and don't engage in the conversation. It is a way of saying "I refuse to participate." When they notice your lack of response, it may encourage them to stop and consider what they are doing. If you don't think you can just sit there and "zip your lip," it's best to remove yourself and chill for a while.

Assert your right to love each parent.
When one parent bad-mouths another, say, "I have a right to love my father/mother (the other parent) and nothing you can say is going to change that." This will not only silence them, but it will also help you to stick up for yourself. Remember, you have just one father and mother. You have a right to love them both. It's what God wants for you, as well.

Ask God for help.
When your parents put you in the battlefield, it's normal to feel confused, guilty, and angry. Both your mom and your dad may want you to take sides, but you can't. You know that neither one of them is all right or all wrong. You want to please them both, but you don't know how. Talking with God will help you find some perspective and stop feeling that it is your responsibility to fix their problems. It also will help you to stay on track, because you will be focusing on what you believe God wants for you to do.

Don't let yourself be manipulated.
Stand your ground and leave the problem in your parents' hands, where it belongs. For example, suppose one parent says, "If your mom/dad goes to your basketball game, I'm not going." Or, "You're going to invite your mom/dad to your recital after all he/she has done to us?" Realize that these are attempts to control you. Don't let yourself be controlled by accepting the guilt

and inviting only one parent to an event. Doing so rewards your parent(s) for bad behavior. Let your parents take responsibility for their own decisions and actions. If your dad/mom doesn't go to your game because your other parent will be there, then he/she is the one who is responsible for that decision, not you. And if your mom/dad tries to lay a guilt trip on you instead of respecting your right to have a relationship with your other parent, then he/she is the one who needs to deal with those feelings on their own.

Try to change the subject while staying positive.
For example, when your mom/dad starts bad-mouthing the other parent, you could say "You know, I don't see you as much as I did before. Let's not let mom/dad interfere in our relationship. Our time together is too important. By the way, did I tell you I made the basketball team?" If the action step you choose doesn't seem to help, try another. Eventually you will find the one that works for you. What's most important is to keep on trying. Only by taking action can you put an end to being placed in the battlefield. Hopefully sooner or later, they will get the hint and not continue to put you in that situation.

Write your parents a letter.
Spell out how his or her actions upset you. Here is a sample letter that might give you some ideas of how to word what you want to say:

> Dear Dad and Mom,
>
> Ever since the separation, I have tried extra-hard to have a good relationship with each of you.
>
> I love you both. However, I now feel like I have to "choose sides" because of all your bad-mouthing. I shouldn't have to hear the details of your marital problems or bear the brunt of your anger. When you put down each other, you put me down too, because I'm part of you both. It really hurts.
> I'm starting to lose respect for you. You're both adults and should know better. This is your separation, not mine.
>
> From now on, I'm going to leave the room if you start saying things that make me feel uncomfortable. I don't want my relationship with either of you to be ruined, but I need you to help me by respecting my love for each of you. This would show me that you really do love me, too.
>
> Love,

A letter is a good way to express your feelings when the words just don't come out or when you're too scared to say them. It is also a way to get your anger out, and remember, you don't have to send the letter. Just getting your words out on paper helps a great deal. Writing a letter to God would be a good idea, too. If you are angry at Him, just tell Him. Remember, He already knows anyway.

Ask a family friend or a relative (who hasn't taken sides) to help you.
This person could take you back and forth to see each parent, or he or she could sit down with all of you and discuss how much the battlefield upsets you. He or she could try to lay out healthy boundaries for all of you. They could also give you some objective advice and pray with you.

Ask your parent to talk with a family counselor.
If your parents don't agree to this, ask to see a counselor yourself, or talk about the situation with an adult whom you trust (for example, a pastor, teacher, guidance counselor, coach, etc.).

The Real Deal

Below is a list of important facts. Check those that you especially need to remember.

_____ I don't have the power to fix Mom and Dad's problems or make them happy; only they do.

_____ Refusing to stay on the battlefield won't cost me my relationship with Mom or Dad. It's good to protect myself and to set boundaries.

_____ No matter how good my intentions are, when I stay on the Battle Field, the only person I'm hurting is me.

_____ I'm doing what's good and loving for myself, and I'm doing what's good and loving for my Mom and Dad.

_____ I shouldn't be afraid to follow my own judgment just because I'm not an adult yet. Teenagers can be right, too. I can seek out an objective person to share my thoughts with.

_____ My job right now is to figure out who I am. This sometimes means separating my thoughts from my parent's so that I can decide my own values, goals, and dreams, along with what God wants for me.

_____ No matter what I feel, I have not done anything to cause this divorce; this is not about me.

_____ God cares about me and wants to help me. He has not forgotten me.

_____ I am not responsible for my parents' arguments. I can only control my own responses.

_____ I need to remember that God cares for me and wants to be there for me. I won't forget to spend time with Him.

_____ I can get beyond this and have a very happy life. My future does not need to be defined by my parent's divorce.

_____ I cannot control the choices my parents make, but I can control my responses to them.

_____ It is not my job to take care of my parents. I have enough other things on my plate. I need to make sure I make healthy choices for me.

Feelings Box

What exactly is a Feelings Toolbox?
It's a collection of your various favorite and healthy items that you can use when you are feeling anxious, panicky, or distressed.

Many therapists recommend that their patients create a "coping toolbox" for those times when they need something to help them get through an anxiety attack, a panic attack, or any other kind of distressing situation.

Below is a list of possible items you can keep in your toolbox. Of course, it's up to you what you add. Just keep in mind that you want to add things that will give you a positive distraction and that will help bring you through difficult times.

Dr. Bach's Rescue Remedies

- Soft blanket
- Tea
- Scented candles
- Gum
- Crossword puzzles
- Anything that smells like lavender
- Hard candy
- Stress ball
- Notecard and pen
- Rubber band to "snap yourself back" into the moment
- A list of affirmations
- Bottle of bubbles
- Protein bar
- Beloved stuffed animal
- Playing cards
- Card from a supportive person
- Pictures of loved ones
- Healing stones and crystals
- iPod loaded with relaxing music
- Pillow
- Pen and notebook to journal
- Running Shoes
- Earplugs
- Water bottle
- Phone

Fill in a Feeling

I hurt _____ when I _____.

I lied when I said, "_____"

I once _____ when I was angry.

It was unsafe for me to _____.

It hurts others when I _____.

I wish I could stop _____.

I am going to try to _____.

I am a _____ person.

I feel bad about _____.

I feel good about _____.

I often worry about _____.

I'm glad that I am _____.

I wish I knew how to _____.

Someday I'm going to _____.

The Big As

A_____. This is the "what." Many times we react to feelings in unhealthy ways because we don't take the time to really identify what we are feeling. Sometimes when we don't become aware of our feelings, we only make things worse by either responding inappropriately or choosing to deny our feelings.

A_____. Once we become aware of what we are facing, we can acknowledge our needs to ourselves and others. We can let go of the chaos and grab control of our emotions. When we allow ourselves to blow up, shut down, or blame ourselves, we are not thinking clearly and we allow the situation to control our responses. Keep in mind, others may not agree or even understand your feelings and needs. But we need to stand up for what we believe before we can move forward.

A_____. This is the simplest but hardest step. Feelings can be painful and sometimes irrational. By allowing yourself the freedom to become aware of and acknowledge your feelings, you are now able to make good choices about what to do next. Start by asking yourself some good questions.

Questions to Ask yourself

What is the best thing to do right now?

Whom do I feel safe talking to this about?

What tools do I need to use to help me make better choices the next time?

What can I do to bring myself some relief?

What do I need to do to make amends with those affected by my choices?

Natural Consequences

Match each behavior with its natural consequence.

BEHAVIOR

_____ Playing "tag" in a parking lot

_____ Stealing money from your friend's room

_____ Teasing a neighborhood dog

_____ Running away from home

_____ Playing with matches

_____ Playing "catch" in the house

_____ Leaving your bike out in the yard all night

_____ Starting a fight with someone smaller than you

_____ Smoking a cigarette

_____ Dropping out of school

_____ Loaning a friend $25

_____ Having a bad attitude

CONSEQUENCE

A. Might break something expensive

B. Might get hit by a car

C. Might not have any friends; people might not like you

D. Might get addicted, could end up getting yellow teeth or even cancer

E. Might lose trust or lose a friend

F. Might get attacked or bitten

G. Might get beaten up or embarrassed

H. It could get stolen

I. Might not get your money back

J. Might not be able to get a good job

K. Could burn the house down; could burn yourself

L. Someone might take advantage of you or hurt you

Feelings Tool Kit

Below are some things to help you work through your feelings. Check any that you have tried. Put a star by any that seem worth a try next time.

Exercise

Much has been written about the benefits that come both emotionally and physically through exercise. Exercise makes us feel better, improves our mood, increases pleasure, and minimizes pain. Exercise can lift your spirits and help you feel better about yourself. It also serves as a good distraction.

Ask Questions

If there is something you don't understand, ask your parent(s) to tell you more about it. It won't take away the hurt, but it may help you understand more of the truth. It might also prevent you from taking sides, blaming yourself, or wishing for things that probably won't come true.

Record Your Feelings and Listen

You might find it easier to talk out your feelings than to write them down. If so, it can help to record what you say, then play it back. Many times you will be surprised at what you said. Not only will it help you feel better, but you might hear something in what you say that needs attention, such as an irrational belief. You can then erase the recording if you want to. It will also help you to realize when you are falling into the pattern of repeating old lies. Once you hear yourself repeating these lies, remind yourself to turn these negative thoughts into more positive ones.

Accept What You Can't Change

Accept the fact that your parents are not perfect and they may make bad choices. Find a positive role model (such as a coach, teacher, youth pastor, aunt, or uncle) to interact with.

We all deserve to have parents who take seriously the job of raising, loving, and protecting us. Unfortunately, though, not all parents accept this responsibility. If you have a parent who makes unhealthy choices time and time again (for example, not keeping promises, not seeing or calling you, not providing for you, etc.), you need to accept what you cannot change about him or her. Look for a positive role model, someone whom you can depend on, who will be your friend. You deserve support in this tough time.

Talk with Someone You Trust

Talking about what you're going through with a close friend or an adult whom you trust is a good way to handle feeling bummed out. Another person can ask helpful questions or share similar experiences that may help you understand your feelings and feel less alone. A school counselor or pastor may have good advice, as well.

Keep a Journal

(for example, write a blog or compose a poem, story, or song about how you feel.)

Negative feelings often become less powerful when you write them out. You don't have to show anyone what you write unless you want to. Give yourself permission to rip up or delete what you have written. The important thing is to express your feelings. These can be personal, and they can even be letters to God. Remember, nothing will surprise Him. He already knows your heart.

Let Yourself Cry

There are all kinds of losses to accept when parents break up. Crying is not a sign of weakness; it is a release of grief. Crying relieves stress, reduces hormone and chemical levels in the body, and can help you return to a calmer state.

Be Creative

Sometimes it is difficult to express your feelings in words. You might find it helpful to get a large pad on which to draw. Don't worry about how it looks. Use shapes and colors and textures to convey your emotions. You may just want to scribble. That's okay, too.

Taking It Home

Toward Yourself... Questions to take to my heart:

> Look into your heart as you answer these questions. This is introspection time — time to grapple with what drives your thinking and behavior. Be sure to "capture your thoughts."

Make yourself a Feelings toolbox and put it in your room to use when you need to release your frustrations.

Have your parents ever made you feel caught in the middle? What happened? What did you do, and how did it make you feel?

Do you have a plan to keep from getting caught in the middle again? Explain your plan. Try it this week if you need to, and be prepared to share with the group how it went.

If I were to give someone an object that would best describe my feelings right now, the object would be a _____.

And I would give it to _____.

Because _____.

Week 7

Taking It Home

Toward Others... Questions to take to others:

> Healing cannot become complete without affecting the lives of those around us. Be courageous and go outside your comfort zone to take a risk and work on your relationships with others. This is application time — time to take what you have learned and apply it to your own individual experience.

Have either of your parents ever tried to use you as a messenger, a spy, or a sounding board? Which one was it and how did that make you feel?

Do you think telling your parents how you feel is being disrespectful? How can you come across in a way that is respectful? (Remember that your tone and non verbal messages can make a huge impact, negatively or positively.)

What are some ways you can explain to your parents how you feel when you are put in the middle? How can you put them into practice?

Being in the middle is an awful place to be. How have you taken steps to protect yourself from ending up there in the future?

Week 7

Taking It Home

Toward God... Questions to take to God:

> When you ask God a question, expect His Spirit to respond to your heart. Be careful not to rush it, or manufacture an answer. Don't jot down your idea of the "right answer." Just pose the question to God, and wait on Him to speak personally to your heart.

Write out four words or phrases below that describe your feelings about God.

1.

2.

3.

4.

Read Colossians 1:10-13. How do you think this passage pertains to your situation?

Below, write a note to God about something that happened this week that really frustrated you. Then leave it with Him and rest in His peace.

Week 7

HELPING CHILDREN DEAL WITH

Symptoms of Sadness

- Crying/Tears
- Loneliness
- Ignoring Past Hobbies
- Fatigue
- Poor Decision Making
- Withdrawal
- Lack of Concentration
- Changes in Eating Habits
- Changes in Sleep Patterns
- Passivity

Sad: Affected by unhappiness or grief; sorrowful or mournful *Dictionary.com*

Ps. 9:9	Is. 25:8
Ps. 22:24	Is. 54:30
Ps. 27:4-5	Lm. 3:31-33
Ps. 30:5	Nah. 1:7
Ps. 34:18	Mt. 5:4
Ps. 37:39	Mt. 11:25-30
Ps. 46:1-2	Jn. 14:27
Ps. 55:22	2 Cor. 1:3-5
Ps 71:20-21	Ph. 4:6
Ps. 73:26	Heb. 4:14-16
Ps. 138:7	1 Pt. 5:6-7
Pr. 14:32	Rev. 21:4

Scripture References

THERE'LL BE SAD SONGS....TO MAKE YOU CRY!!! As parents, one of the things we hate the most is to see our kids sad. We will do all that we can to make keep our kids from being sad and to cheer them up when they are sad. Unfortunately, just trying to make a child happy again fails to allow them the time to deal with whatever is causing the sadness in the first place. Children are often left wanting to blame someone for the sadness they are feeling, and those closest to them frequently become the targets of that blame. Many kids will also seek to mask their sadness, particularly from parents, so as not to be a "further burden."

What To Say/Do

- "Sometimes I get really sad too."
- "What can you do to make this situation better?"
- "I love you and God loves you."
- "You're not alone in this."
- "You are important to me."
- "Do you want a hug?"
- "I can't really understand what you're feeling, but I'm here for you."
- "I'm not going to leave or abandon you."

What NOT To Say/Do

- Don't dismiss the feeling.
- "No one ever said life was fair."
- "Just think positive."
- "You're one messed up kid."
- "Stop feeling sorry for yourself."
- "Snap out of it."
- "It's your own fault."
- "There are lots of people worse off than you are."
- "Just hang in there, it'll pass."

http://Hope4HurtingKids.com

© 2017

Between Two Worlds

**Lesson Eight
Week 8**

GOALS

This week we want to:
1. Learn to expect, accept, and adapt to changes
2. Create a timeline and identify the changes taking place in your life
3. Compare differences and find ways to embrace new changes
4. Learn ways to manage the stress that change can bring
5. Adjust and learn to live and prosper in your single-parent home
6. Evaluate the stresses in your life
7. Review the "Taking It Home" Assignments

Verses of the week:

"When I am afraid, I put my trust in you. In God, whose word I praise—in God I trust and am not afraid."

Psalm 56:3–4

SOMETHING TO THINK ABOUT

It's not easy moving from a two-parent home to a single-parent household. Everything changes. Not only do you miss one parent when you are with the other, but nothing stays the same. You may feel like you are being split in two. The thing about change is that it is going to happen, whether you are ready for it or not, so you might as well find ways to accept it and make the best of it. We will be exploring the numerous changes you are experiencing in this situation and discover practical ways to cope while you are adapting to your new way of life. This process is never easy. But the more resistant we are to change, the more difficult the process will be. Let's agree to move through these changes together and find ways to embrace our new family situations.

Be Blessed!

"My God will meet all your needs according to the riches of his glory in Christ Jesus."

Philippians 4:19

Timeline of My Life

Starting from when you were a baby, draw pictures along this timeline that represent major events in your life, such as your parents' divorce, moving to a new house or school, or acquiring a stepfamily.

Ideas to get you started

My Story Today

Changes in My Life

Your parents' decision to separate or divorce will bring about many changes in your life. Many of them you will not like, and you may feel like you have no control over them. Mark the areas of change that you have experienced.

- ☐ Home
- ☐ Time together
- ☐ Money
- ☐ Freedom
- ☐ Sports
- ☐ A stepparent
- ☐ Family
- ☐ Free time

- ☐ Fights
- ☐ Bedtimes
- ☐ Clothing
- ☐ Vacations
- ☐ School
- ☐ Friends
- ☐ Responsibilities
- ☐ Neighbors

- ☐ Youth group
- ☐ Holidays
- ☐ Church
- ☐ Food
- ☐ Rules
- ☐ Siblings
- ☐ Mom's name
- ☐ Other: _____

Thoughts to Consider

The biggest change I fear most and why: _____
_____
_____

The best change I have experienced so far: _____
_____
_____

The most difficult change for me has been: _____
_____
_____

How I feel about this change: _____
_____
_____

STRESS CHALLENGE

Below is a list of stressful events that may have taken place in your life. They have different number values to show the amount of pressure that each adds to your life. Sit back, take a moment, and review your life over the past two years. Go through the following list. Circle the stressful events that have happened or are currently taking place in your life. When you are done add up the total to see what your Life Stress Score is.

Event	Score	Event	Score
Parent died	98	Discovered being an adopted child	63
Brother or sister died	95	Parent married a stepparent	63
Close friend died	92	Had trouble with teacher or principal	63
Unwed pregnancy	92	Had problems with acne, weight, or height	63
Parents divorced	86	Had a serious illness requiring hospitalization	58
Failed one or more subjects at school	85	Attended a new school	57
Arrested by the police	84	Did not make cut for an extracurricular activity	55
Flunked a grade of school	83	Moved to a new home	51
Family member had trouble with alcohol	79	Began to date	51
Took drugs or drank alcohol	77	Suspended from school	50
Lost a favorite pet	77	Brother or sister born	50
Fathered an unwed pregnancy	77	Increased arguments between parents	48
Parent or relative got very sick	77	Had change in physical appearance (braces, eyeglasses)	47
Parent received jail sentence	75	Hassled with a brother or sister	46
Lost a job	74	Experienced change in parents' financial status	45
Broke up with a girl/boyfriend	74	Started menstrual period	45
Quit school	73	Became a senior in high school	42
Parents became separated	69	Had increased absence of parent from home	38
Close friend became pregnant	69	Had someone new move in with your family	35
Parent lost job	69	Started a job	34
Change in the acceptance by peers	67	Mother got pregnant	31
Pregnancy of unwed sister	64	Made new friends	27
Became very sick or badly hurt	64	Brother or sister got married	26
Hassled with parents	64		

Total Score: _____

A score of 300 points or more is a sign that you are at great risk of severe illness and high anxiety. Eighty percent of people who score 300 points or more will get some sort of illness due to stress. A score between 150 and 299, causes people to have a 50 percent chance of getting sick. People with less than 150 have only 30 percent chance of getting sick.

The important point is that you can significantly decrease your chances of serious illness and high anxiety by decreasing the amount of stress in your life. You can control much of the change that occurs. In addition, by anticipating changes and planning for them, you are more prepared to handle them and your stress level decreases immensely.

Additional Stress Relief

Look at the list of events. Break them into two groups.

1. Those you may be able to control the severity of.
2. Those you cannot control. The more you face these challenges and prepare for their impact, the less stress they will have on your life.

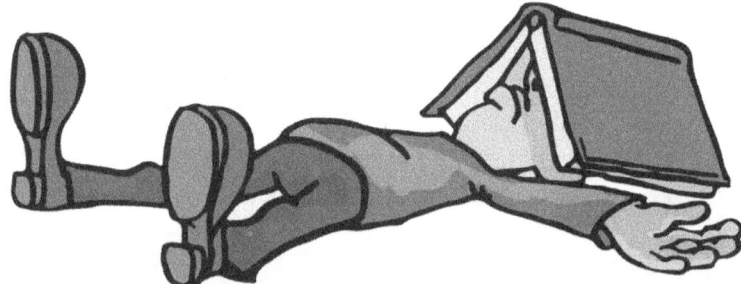

*Test is from Mental Health of America

What's the Difference?

1. What are some things that have changed since living in a single-parent home, as compared to the two-parent world you were used to?

2. In what ways are things the same as when you were living in the same home?

3. What do you miss most about your parents not living together?

4. How did you respond when you found out or were told that your parents were separating or getting a divorce?

5. How did they tell you?

6. What did your parents do to help you feel better?

7. Did anybody else do anything to try to make you feel better?

8. Did you cry? Why or why not? Have you cried since that time? Do you think it helps to cry?

9. Did you get angry? Whom were you angry with and why?

Difficult Changes

1. Have both of your parents had to work outside the home? Is this different than things were before the separation?

2. Have you noticed a change in how money is spent in your home since the separation?

3. Are there any things that you used to get or do prior to the separation that you cannot afford anymore? What are they?

4. What are some things you have had to accept that your family will not be able to afford right now?

5. Have you had to sell anything? If so, what? Was it hard for you to do?

6. Has your family had to sell their home because of the divorce?

7. Have you had to move into a different place because of the divorce?

8. How did you feel about the move?

9. If you have moved or are going to be moving soon, do you think the new place will be better than the old one, or not as good? Why or why not?

10. What is one thing you miss about your old home?

11. What is one thing you like or will like about your new home?

Dealing with Mom and Dad

Note: Depending on which parent is your primary guardian, you may need to substitute your mom or your dad for these questions.

Dealing with Mom

(Assuming your mom is your primary caregiver; if not, substitute your dad)

What are some of the changes and conflicts you have experienced with your mom as a single parent?

Learning to communicate and compromise with your mom rather than reacting out of your anger or giving up is a significant skill to learn. How can you help in communicating?

Sometimes mom may try to be your best friend. She may let you come and go as you please and doesn't make you do any work around the house. What should you do if this is your mom?

Dealing with Dad

(Assuming your dad is your primary caregiver; if not, substitute your mom)

What are some of the challenges you face in relating to your noncustodial parent?

Sometimes the noncustodial parent tries to appease their guilt by constantly showing the kids a good time or buying them things. What should you do if this is a common occurrence?

Sometimes the parent never really learns how to be a single parent and often expects you to fulfill that role. What should you do if this occurs in your family?

Have you made a place of your own at your noncustodial parent's house where you can keep a few personal things that make it feel a little more like home?

Personal Child Visitation Wishes

Note: Keep in mind that your parenting visitation agreement is ultimately your parents' decision, but take a minute to consider how you would like it to look.

I would like to live with my mother _____ days a week.

I would like to live with my father _____ days a week.

I would like to live with _____, _____ days a week.

I feel safe with my mom _____, and with my dad _____.

I would like to be able to call my mom more often: _____.

I would like to be able to call my dad more often: _____.

I would like to be able to call my grandparents more often: _____.

I would like to attend _____ school.

I would like to attend _____ church.

My favorite activities I would like to do with my mother:.   My favorite activities I would like to do with my father:.
_____   _____
_____   _____
_____   _____

Some things I would change about my mom are: Some things I would change about my dad are:
_____   _____
_____   _____
_____   _____

Additional Comments or Wishes:

 # A Letter from a Child of Divorce

Dear Mom and Dad,

I realize something is happening, but I don't really know what it is. Life is different, and I'm scared to death and unsure of my future. Here's what I need from you, my parents:

- ♥ I need both of you to stay involved in my life. When I'm not with you, please write letters, make phone calls, and ask me lots of questions. When you don't stay involved and I don't hear from you, I feel like I'm not important and that you don't really love me.

- ♥ I need to see you. Make time for me, no matter how far apart we are, how busy you are or what your finances are like.

- ♥ I miss you when we're not together. When you're out of sight, I think you've forgotten me and don't love me.

- ♥ I need you to please stop fighting and work harder to get along with each other. Figure out how to agree on matters related to me. When you fight about me, I think that I did something wrong, and I feel guilty.

- ♥ I need to feel like it is okay to love you both. I need to feel like it is okay to enjoy the time that I spend with each of you. Please support me and the time that I spend with each of you. If you act jealous or upset, I feel like I need to take sides and love one parent more than the other.

- ♥ I need you to find a way to positively and directly communicate directly with each other about me, and the things I need or want. Please don't put me in the middle or make me be your messenger.

- ♥ I need you to say only nice things about each other in front of me, because I am half of both of you and I love both of you equally. When you say mean, unkind things about my other parent, I feel like you don't like them, and therefore, you don't like me. I also feel like you are putting me in the middle and asking me to choose one of you over the other.

I need both of my parents. Please remember that I want both of you to be a part of my life. I count on both my mom and my dad to raise me, to teach me what is important, and to help me when I have problems.

Thank you.

Love, Your Child

Taking It Home

Toward Yourself... Questions to take to my heart:

> Look into your heart as you answer these questions. This is introspection time — time to grapple with what drives your thinking and behavior. Be sure to "capture your thoughts."

Which five words would best describe your family right now?

If you could change one thing about your family, what would it be?

You may feel opposite feelings sometimes — like being really angry at someone and also loving and missing them at the same time. List some of the "opposites" that you feel.

Do you have different rules at Mom's house than you do at Dad's house? How do you handle that?

Do you share what you do at one parent's home with the other parent? Are you supposed to? If so, how much?

How do you think your parents are going to change as a result of the divorce?

Week 8

Taking It Home

Toward Others... Questions to take to others:

> Healing cannot become complete without affecting the lives of those around us. Be courageous and go outside your comfort zone to take a risk and work on your relationships with others. This is application time — time to take what you have learned and apply it to your own individual experience.

Is it hard to talk to your parents about your feelings concerning your visitation schedule? Why or why not?

What is one thing you wish you could share with your parents?

What are the best parts about your relationship with your mom?

What are the worst parts about your relationship with your mom?

Rate your relationship with your mom with 1 being no relationship at all and 10 being the best possible relationship.

    1   2   3   4   5   6   7   8   9   10

What are the best parts about your relationship with your dad?

What are the worst parts about your relationship with your dad?

Rate your relationship with your dad with 1 being no relationship at all and 10 being the best possible relationship.

    1   2   3   4   5   6   7   8   9   10

Week 8

Taking It Home

Toward God... Questions to take to God:

> When you ask God a question, expect His Spirit to respond to your heart. Be careful not to rush it, or manufacture an answer. Don't jot down your idea of the "right answer." Just pose the question to God, and wait on Him to speak personally to your heart.

What things make you feel safe and secure?

What things make you feel scared?

When do you feel most alone?

Read Hebrews 13:5. Who will never leave you nor forsake you? Do you believe that promise?

Read Deuteronomy 31:6 and write it out below. What does it mean to you?

What changes do you need to lay at the feet of Jesus because you just can't accept them on your own?

Week 8

When One Becomes Two

**Lesson Nine
Week 9**

GOALS

This week we want to:
1. Start, if you haven't already, to entertain the thought of your parents dating other people
2. Look at the differences between a single-parent home and that of a stepfamily
3. Become more open-minded about different ways to view situations in other people's eyes
4. Find ways to resolve conflict within your family unit
5. Discover new ways to build relationships instead of building walls in your stepfamily home
6. Review the "Taking It Home" assignments

Verses of the week:

"Do not conform to the pattern of this world, but be transformed by the renewing of your mind. Then you will be able to test and approve what God's will is—his good, pleasing and perfect will."

Romans 12:2

SOMETHING TO THINK ABOUT

Dating? New relationships? What next? This stage can be very difficult on everyone. What are you supposed to say? How are you expected to act? Try to enter this stage with your eyes open and your heart ready to consider new relationships. The more opportunities you have to share your feelings with your parents, the better this transition will be. If or when the day comes when one or both of your parents remarry, we hope you will use all of the tools you have learned here to help you adjust. Blending families can be very tricky. Keep in mind that you could gain even more good relationships if you work with it, not against it. What do you have to lose? It's worth the risk.

Be Blessed!

"...being strengthened with all power according to his glorious might so that you may have great endurance and patience."

Colossians 1:11

The Bumpy Road

Below are some ways in which families may change after a separation or divorce. Check the ones that describe your family. When you're finished, go back and put a star by the changes that are the toughest for you.

- [ ] We moved to a different home. I live in two different homes now.
- [ ] I have less time now with one or both of my parents.
- [ ] My parents are not like themselves anymore. (Examples: Mom/Dad is always crying, yelling, or doing something unhealthy, like abusing drugs or alcohol.)
- [ ] We don't do things as a family anymore. I miss being together as a family.
- [ ] We have less money. I can't get as many clothes or go out with my friends as much anymore.
- [ ] One (or both) of my parents has started dating or has remarried.
- [ ] My parents are putting me in the middle of their fights.
- [ ] My mom no longer uses her married name, so we have different last names.
- [ ] The parent I'm living with works longer hours or has gone back to school.
- [ ] I have to do more chores now.
- [ ] I had to get a job.
- [ ] I don't understand whats going on. My parents keep secrets or never give me a straight answer.
- [ ] I have to take care of my younger siblings more.
- [ ] My friends don't live near me anymore.
- [ ] My rules and responsibilities have changed.
- [ ] I have to share a bedroom now.
- [ ] I had to change schools.
- [ ] I had to change churches and/or youth groups.
- [ ] Other:_____

My Family

List all of your family members, how they are related to you, and one specific thing you like to do with each of them.

Name	Relationship	Activity

The thing that is most different from my original family is:
_____
_____

The best thing about our stepfamily is:
_____
_____

The most difficult thing about our stepfamily is:
_____
_____

We argue a lot about:
_____
_____

One thing I would change is:
_____
_____

I really like it when we:
_____
_____

I wish my new stepparent knew this about me:
_____
_____

My favorite memory as a stepfamily so far is:
_____
_____

The biggest change when we became a stepfamily was:
_____
_____

In our family birth order, I went from the _____ in the family to the _____.

The hardest part of that has been:
_____

Weights That Matter!

Decode the words below to reveal the Weights That Matter in our lives!

A	B	C	D	E	F	G	H	I
∾	♥	✿	☾	⊙	△	✱	✳	»

J	K	L	M	N	O	P	Q
≡	•	ξ	❀	¤	☺	♪	☀

R	S	T	U	V	W	X	Y	Z
♦	⌘	✎	⎈	▩	☆	☏	♣	☠

1. LOVE
2. GRACE
3. JOY
4. KINDNESS
5. PEACE
6. SELFCONTROL
7. GENEROSITY
8. PATIENCE

Step by Step

Take a look at your stepfamily relationships. It is important to be intentional about building relationships instead of walls. Across the top are the weights that matter that we discussed earlier. On the left are the people in your stepfamily. Think of ways you can display each characteristic to the different people in your stepfamily.

	Love	Patience	Grace	Peace	Joy	Kindness	Self-Control	Generosity
Mom/Dad								
Stepdad/Stepmom								
Sibling								
Sibling								
Stepsibling								
Stepsibling								
Half sibling								

Taking It Home

Toward Yourself... Questions to take to my heart:

> Look into your heart as you answer these questions. This is introspection time — time to grapple with what drives your thinking and behavior. Be sure to "capture your thoughts."

Are you ready for your mom to start dating? What would you say if she asked you if it was okay? If she is dating now, how do you feel about it?

Are you ready for your dad to start dating? What would you say if he asked you if it was okay? If he is dating now, how do you feel about it?

If either or both of your parents are dating, do you like their boyfriend/girlfriend, or your stepmom or stepdad? List two things you like about them.

1. _____
2. _____

If either or both of your parents have remarried, how did you respond when you first heard that they were going to marry someone else? Have things gotten any better?

Week 9

Taking It Home

Toward Others... Questions to take to others:

> Healing cannot become complete without affecting the lives of those around us. Be courageous and go outside your comfort zone to take a risk and work on your relationships with others. This is application time — time to take what you have learned and apply it to your individual experience.

Do you think your mom or dad should tell you when and whom they are dating? Have you talked about it?

If one of your parents has remarried, has your relationship with that parent gotten better or worse? In what ways?

Has this parent gained anything positive from his or her new relationship, or do you feel it has been a negative experience?

If you are now living in a stepfamily, what has changed now that your parent has gotten remarried?

How is your new stepfamily similar to or different from your original family?

Do you feel as if you have a "family" again? If not, explain why.

Week 9

Taking It Home

Toward God... Questions to take to God:

> When you ask God a question, expect His Spirit to respond to your heart. Be careful not to rush it, or manufacture an answer. Don't jot down your idea of the "right answer." Just pose the question to God, and wait on Him to speak personally to your heart.

Do you think God will bless your new family, or do you think He views your family as "broken"?

Do you feel as if God wants you to accept this new family in your life? If so, what would that look like?

In what ways can God help you deal with the frustrations that the creation of a stepfamily can bring?

How do you think God could use you in this new stepfamily?

Week 9

HELPING CHILDREN DEAL WITH

Causes of Anxiety in Kids

- Arguments
- Guilt
- School
- Bullying
- Fear for parents
- Fitting in
- Appearance
- Money
- Abandonment
- Parents Splitting Up
- Being teased
- Getting in trouble
- Safety

Anxiety: Distress or uneasiness of the mind caused by fear of danger or misfortune. *Dictionary.com*

Dt. 3:22	Mt. 6:25-34
Dt. 31:8	Mt. 10:31
Neh. 8:10	Mt. 11:28
Ps 23:4	Jn 14:27
Ps. 34:4	Jn. 16:33
Ps. 46:10	Rom. 8:31
Ps. 55:22-23	Phil. 4:6-7
Prov. 3:5-8	Phil. 4:19
Prov. 12:25	Heb. 13:6
Is. 41:10	1 Pt. 5:6-7

Scripture References

ANXIETY...A SILENT KILLER! Worry is a normal part of everyday life, but when that worry interferes with a child's ability to accomplish normal everyday tasks it has risen to the level of anxiety. Children can suffer from separation anxiety, social anxiety, panic attacks or may simply have an unexplainable fear of some bad thing which is "bound to happen." Many anxious children may be quiet and complacent leading them to suffer in silence. Prolonged periods of anxiety can lead to chronic illness. The key to helping children deal with anxiety is information. Imagination feeds anxiety, so provide them with as much information as reasonably possible.

What To Say/Do

- "We'll get through this together."
- "I know this is hard."
- "Tell me about it."
- Encourage them to face fears, not run away.
- Let them know that it's ok not be perfect.
- "I love you. You are safe."
- "I get anxious sometimes too. It's no fun."

What NOT To Say/Do

- "This isn't a big deal. Don't worry so much!"
- "Stop being such a worrier."
- "Here are all the reasons you don't have to worry about this."
- "It's going to be ok. Trust me!"
- "What's wrong with you?"
- "That's such a silly thing to be worried about."
- "Get over it."

http://Hope4HurtingKids.com

© 2017

The Missing Link

**Lesson Ten
Week 10**

GOALS

This week we want to:
1. Understand what forgiveness is and what it isn't
2. Forgive yourself and others
3. Understand what repentance looks like
4. Lay your hurts at the cross
5. Learn how to walk in forgiveness every day
6. Review the "Taking It Home" assignments

Verse of the week:

"If we confess our sins, he is faithful and just and will forgive us our sins and purify us from all unrighteousness."

1 John 1:9

SOMETHING TO THINK ABOUT

Forgiveness is tough to wrap your head around. It's hard to give and it's sometimes hard to receive. The key to forgiveness is that it is not a feeling; it is a decision. But along with the decision comes a need to let go and let God deal with the situation or person. It is hard for us to let go, because we want to see remorse, gain better insight, or receive gratification. But how would we feel if God decided to wait to forgive us until we got our own act together?

Being willing to forgive is the first step. Surrender your willingness to God, and He will start to soften your heart. As tough as forgiveness is, forgiveness is the whole basis of our salvation. Without forgiveness, what hope would we have?

Our prayer for you this week is that you would be able to understand the true meaning of forgiveness, experience for yourself the true forgiveness that comes only from Jesus Christ, and then receive the true freedom that comes from letting it go.

Be Blessed!

"Bear with each other and forgive one another if any of you has a grievance against someone. Forgive as the Lord forgave you."

Colossians 3:13

Forgiveness Facts

Circle "True" or "False" for each statement.

- Forgiving someone means that you will no longer get angry or have any more negative feelings toward him or her.
  True   False

- You may want to forgive someone, but you may not be ready on the inside.
  True   False

- If you forgive, you have to put it all behind you, leave it in the past, and become friends with the person who hurt you.
  True   False

- When you forgive others, you believe and accept that God has forgiven you.
  True   False

- Forgiveness is based on a feeling you get telling you that you are ready to move on; until then, you are not ready to forgive.
  True   False

- If you forgive someone, you have to forget what they've done.
  True   False

- You cannot forgive until the offender asks for forgiveness or shows that he or she is sorry.
  True   False

- Forgiving is necessary in the healing process, and you will not be able to completely heal until you do so.
  True   False

- Forgiveness is unconditional.
  True   False

- Forgiveness depends on getting a guarantee that someone won't do the same wrong thing again.
  True   False

- Forgiveness excuses the other person's sin or wrongdoing.
  True   False

- You do not have to forgive an immoral person.
  True   False

Why should we forgive?

1. Because Jesus _____ us (Eph. 4:32; Luke 23:34).

2. Because it frees us from _____ (Heb. 12:14–15).

3. Because it demonstrates Christ's _____ (Col. 3:12–13).

4. Because it will deliver us from Satan's _____ (2 Cor. 2:9–11).

5. Because it delivers us from the _____ from God (Luke 6:35–37).

6. Because if we expect to be forgiven, we ourselves need to _____ (James 2:13).

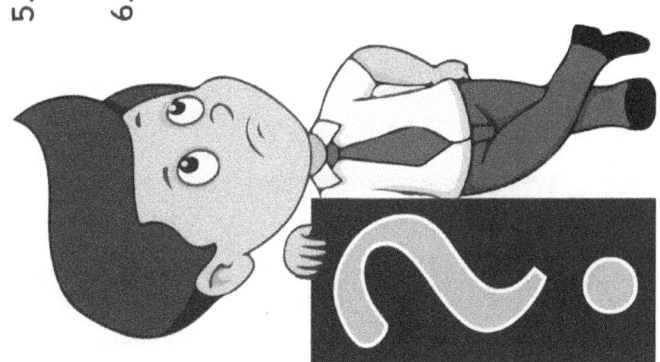

10-Step Forgiveness Exercise

1 Make a list of all the people whom you feel have wronged you in some way. Write down what each one did and why it hurt you.
_____ _____ _____ _____

2 Acknowledge that those things did happen, and that they did hurt you.

3 Make a commitment to yourself to do what you need to do in order not to allow their actions to dictate your belief system about yourself.

4 Recognize that your distress is not coming from what actually happened, but from the thoughts that you have about what happened. Remind yourself that your thoughts are within your control.

5 When you feel yourself again getting upset over what happened, practice the stress-reduction techniques that we learned in Chapter 6 to calm your body's fight-or-flight response.

6 Reprogram your brain to be thankful. Ask yourself, "What am I thankful for?" Ask this repeatedly until you start to feel better.

7 Put your energy into looking for ways to achieve your goals, instead of wasting your energy continuously reliving the negative experiences in your mind.

8 Know that the best response to pain caused by others wrongdoings is a life well-lived. Forgiveness is about taking back your own power.

9 If someone else continues to hurt you, you may need to put up boundaries around their ability to affect your life. This would be good to seek other's advice about. Boundaries can look very different, but they can be very effective if set correctly.

10 Remember that God has forgiven you. We do not deserve His grace and forgiveness, but He continues to forgive us. We should continue to search for ways to extend that same grace to others.

Dear Merciful Father,

Thank You for Your gift of forgiveness. Your only Son loved me enough to come to earth and experience the worst pain imaginable so that I could be forgiven. Your mercy flows to me in spite of my continual faults and failures. Help me to demonstrate that same kind of unconditional love to others, even those who have hurt me.

I understand that even though I feel scarred, my emotions don't have to control my actions. Father, may Your sweet words saturate my mind and direct my thoughts. Help me release the hurt and begin to love as Jesus loves. I want to see my offender through my Savior's eyes. If I can be forgiven, so can he or she.

When I forgive in my words, allow Your Holy Spirit to fill my heart with peace. I pray the peace that only comes from Jesus will rule in my heart, keeping out doubt and questions. I will continue to be grateful for all You have done for me and given to me. With gratitude, I can draw closer to You and let go of unforgiveness. With gratitude, I can see the person who caused my pain as a child of God, loved and accepted. Help me find the compassion that comes with true forgiveness.

And when I see the people who have hurt me, bring this prayer back to my remembrance so I can take any ungodly thoughts captive and keep my heart and mind only on You. I thank You for the work You are doing in my life.

Amen

Colossians 3:13
"Bear with each other and forgive one another if any of you has a grievance against someone. Forgive as the Lord forgave you."

What Is Your Forgiveness IQ?

It's not easy to forgive when you feel slighted or wronged, yet we know that the inability to forgive makes us hold on to bitterness and negativity. For some, forgiving oneself for past actions and choices proves to be the most challenging task of all. It is important to keep in mind that forgiveness is a choice. The first step is to identify important elements of forgiveness, so you can tap in to the healing power of forgiveness and boost your Forgiveness IQ.

For the following 10 questions, rate each item from 1 to 10 to learn your Forgiveness IQ.

```
         1    2    3    4    5    6    7    8    9    10
Strongly Disagree                                Strongly Agree
```

1. _____ I will not forgive someone if they are not sorry and admit what they have done.

2. _____ Those who have wronged or slighted me but take no responsibility for hurting me do not deserve to be forgiven.

3. _____ I find that my lack of ability to forgive keeps me stuck in thinking about what happened in the past.

4. _____ I cannot forgive because I do not want to condone bad behavior.

5. _____ Difficulty in forgiving makes it hard for me to trust others.

6. _____ It is hard to forgive, because forgiving is letting someone off the hook and makes them no longer accountable for what they have done.

7. _____ Forgiveness is something that you just feel, not a trainable skill.

8. _____ Since there's nothing I can do about things now, I keep my hurt feelings to myself

9. _____ If I forgive, that means I will be Vulnerable again so I need to protect myself.

10. _____ I cannot forgive myself for past mistakes, choices, and failures.

Total Score: _____

How Did You Do?

The lower your score, the higher your Forgiveness IQ is.

15 or lower – FORGIVENESS GENIUS – Congratulations! You are a forgiveness expert.

16-29 – FORGIVENESS MASTER – You have given yourself the gift of forgiveness and stay positive.

30-49 – FORGIVENESS PRO – You are generally forgiving and choose acceptance over bitterness.

50-69 – FORGIVENESS INTERMEDIATE – A difficulty with forgiveness has limited your ability to stay positive.

70-84 – FORGIVENESS IMPAIRED – Consider seeking professional help to leave bitterness behind.

85-100 – DANGER ZONE! – A lack of forgiveness impairs your mental health and keeps you stuck. Get help!

FIVE Rs OF REPENTANCE

Know and accept what you did. _____

Feel sorry for what you did. _____

Confess and ask for forgiveness. _____

Make the wrong right. _____

Never do it again. _____

Romans 3:23

"For all have sinned and fall short of the glory of God, and all are justified freely by his grace through the redemption that came by Christ Jesus. God presented Christ as a sacrifice of atonement, through the shedding of his blood – to be received by faith."

Dear Jesus,

Thank You for dying on the cross to forgive me of my sins. I have not only sinned against You, but I have sinned against those I love. I ask for You to please forgive me for _____. I am very sorry I have hurt You, myself, and others by the choices I made. As I repent and choose to turn away from these sins to You, I commit to do my best to live a life pure and clean before You. Thank You for loving me enough to sacrifice Your Son so that I might be forgiven.

Amen

Forgiveness Is Tough

How difficult is it for you to forgive your parents for their separation/divorce or how they are treating you? Check all the statements below that apply to you. Then put a star by your number-one reason.

Forgiving my parents is tough for me because...

⬡ Nothing will change and I'll probably just get hurt again.

⬡ I don't think my mom/dad deserves to be forgiven for what they've done.

⬡ My mom/dad is clueless and doesn't care about how I feel.

⬡ I don't want to face the fact that my mom/dad has made mistakes.

⬡ I want to look up to my parents and be proud of them.

⬡ My mom/dad keeps hurting me over and over again. Why forgive him/her when he/she is just going to do it again?

⬡ I don't really care. It's their problem. I don't need to forgive anyone. I'll take care of myself.

⬡ My parents act as if this is "no big deal." My whole life has been turned upside down!

⬡ I'm so angry that I have no room for forgiveness.

⬡ Other: _____
_____.

Taking It Home

Toward Yourself... Questions to take to my heart:

> Look into your heart as you answer these questions. This is introspection time — time to grapple with what drives your thinking and behavior. Be sure to "capture your thoughts."

What have you been holding on to that has made it hard to forgive and let go?

What new truth did you learn about forgiveness this week?

How did it feel when you forgave someone who hurt you?

Sometimes forgiving ourselves is the hardest thing to do. Are there things for which you need to forgive yourself? If so, what are they?

If someone keeps hurting you, what are some boundaries you can put up to protect yourself in the future?

Week 10

Taking It Home

Toward Others... Questions to take to others:

> Healing cannot become complete without affecting the lives of those around us. Be courageous and go outside your comfort zone to take a risk and work on your relationships with others. This is application time — time to take what you have learned and apply it to your own individual expereince.

Have you completely forgiven your parents for the divorce, or are there things you still need to work through? If so, what are they? Are you working toward forgiveness? Have you started praying for them?

Are there other things you need to forgive them for since the divorce? In what ways have they hurt or frustrated you that has caused a wedge in your relationship?

How have your relationships changed since you've extended forgiveness?

Once you've forgiven, are you committed to these four things?
- Not to dwell on the wrongs anymore?
- Not to bring them up in conversation anymore?
- Not to gossip about them?
- Not to hold their failures against them anymore?

Week 10

Taking It Home

Toward God... Questions to take to God:

> When you ask God a question, expect His Spirit to respond to your heart. Be careful not to rush it, or manufacture an answer. Don't jot down your idea of the "right answer." Just pose the question to God, and wait on Him to speak personally to your heart.

Are there still areas in your life for which you still need to seek forgiveness from God?

Describe a time when you experienced God's forgiveness even though you didn't deserve it. How did it feel?

If you are still holding on to hurts and wrongs from others, are you willing to start praying for those who have hurt you?

What is the hardest truth for you to accept about God's forgiveness?

Week 10

The End of the Journey

**Lesson Eleven
Week 11**

GOALS

This week we want to:
1. Talk about choices—good and bad. Which will you choose?
2. Explore what acceptance looks like on The Roller Coaster of Grief
3. Create life goals for yourself
4. Develop the S.M.A.R.T. goal process
5. Come up with three-month goals
6. Learn tools to help you continue the healing process and reach your goals
7. Review the "Taking It Home" assignments

Verses of the week:

"The LORD will again delight in you and make you prosperous, just as he delighted in your ancestors, if you obey the LORD your God and keep his commands and decrees that are written in this Book of the Law and turn to the LORD your God with all your heart and with all your soul."

Deuteronomy 30:9–10

Be Blessed!

"All these blessings will come upon you and accompany you if you obey the LORD your God."

Deuteronomy 28:2

SOMETHING TO THINK ABOUT

As you reach the point of acceptance, realize that you will continue to have many choices to make. Each choice will determine whether you will continue one step closer to healing or take one step further back into pain. As situations and other changes come up, you will need to process your responses, but hopefully by having gone through this class, you will be able to make healthy choices that lead to freedom.

Setting goals is an intentional way to help you move toward acceptance and keep your focus on your future. Take the time necessary to periodically evaluate and redefine your goals. Your success will be determined by the effort you put into this process. Your future is worth the effort.

ACCEPTANCE

A= _____ Accepting your reality as it exists for you right now; what it is and not what you think it should or could be.

C= _____ The challenges of a child from a divorced family is much more complex than those of children from intact families. You will have a more difficult time with intimacy, trust, commitment, loyalty, and passion.

C= _____ Divorce causes major changes in the lives of children of divorce. Witnessing the loss of love between parents, having parents break their marriage commitment, adjusting to going back and forth between two homes, and the daily absence of one parent while living with the other all cause major life changes.

E= _____ Children raised in divorced families tend to have a less positive attitude toward their own marriages and thus have false expectations for relationships of their own someday.

P= _____ Grief is a process that everyone goes through when they experience a loss. It is a journey through understanding and dealing with what happened. The goal of the grieving process is to reach an acceptance of the loss that will allow you to move on with your life. Grief is not an easy process, but it is a necessary part of healing.

T= _____ Healthy relationships are built on trust; however, many children of divorced parents struggle with trust when working through their own relationship challenges.

A= _____ It is important to identify and acknowledge your feelings related to your parents' separation/divorce. By acknowledging your hurts and feelings, you are opening yourself up to healing. You will never reach the stage of acceptance if you don't first acknowledge your feelings.

N= _____ Going through a family divorce changes not only your surroundings and circumstances, but it also changes who you are. Do the work to become a better YOU.

C= _____ The choice is yours. You can choose to grow through this experience or allow it to rob you of a positive future. And just as you have a choice in how you handle your parents' divorce, you now have a choice in your walk with God and in making good choices that will affect your future relationships.

E= _____ As hard as this experience has been for you, you now have an opportunity to encourage and help others who may be going through the same heartache. Despite the pain of your past, with God you can face the future.

SMART GOALS

When it comes to setting goals, a useful acronym to remember is S.M.A.R.T.

_____: A specific goal has a much greater chance of being accomplished than a general goal. To set a specific goal, you must answer the six "W" questions.

Who?   What?   Why?   Where?   When?   Which?

_____: Establish criteria for measuring progress toward the attainment of each goal you set. When you measure your progress, you stay on track, reach your target dates, and experience the joy of achieving your goals.

Ask yourself:

How will I know when the result has been achieved?

How will I verify the achievement of this goal?

_____: When you identify a goal, write it out, and make a plan, you are setting an attainable goal. You will see opportunities arise that will help you in accomplishing this goal. You will develop a positive attitude working toward an attainable goal, and you will develop traits that will give you the strength to see it through.

_____: To be realistic, a goal needs to be something you are both willing and able to accomplish. A goal can be both high and realistic; you are the only one who can decide just how high your goal should be. But be sure that every goal represents substantial progress.

_____: Time creates a sense of urgency. Knowing you have to accomplish a task by a certain time makes you accountable. Know what those timelines are. Understand what needs to be done by when, and take the steps necessary to meet those timelines.

Setting Life Goals

For each category listed below, write down the things you are doing well, and the areas where you need improvement. Then write a goal or two for each category.

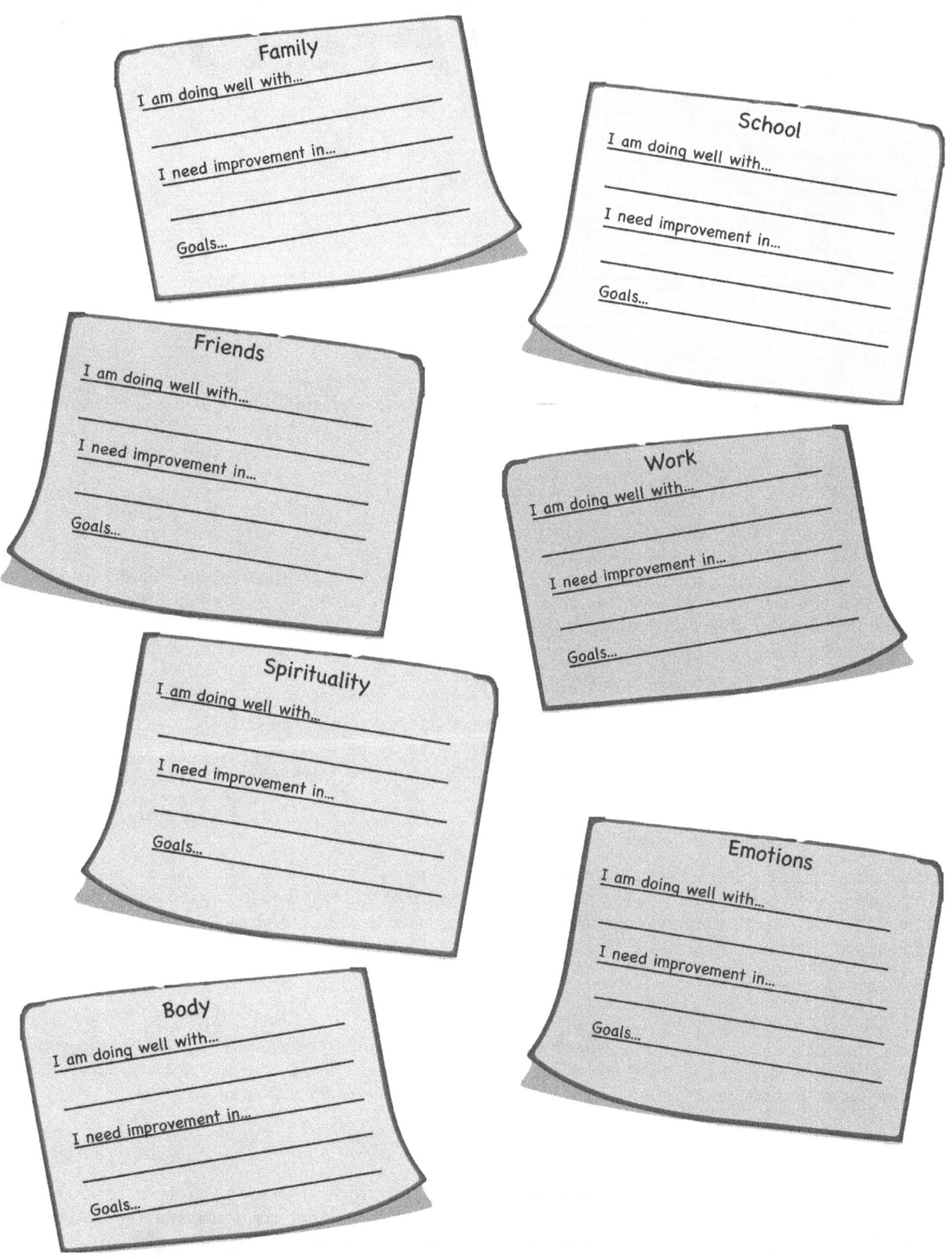

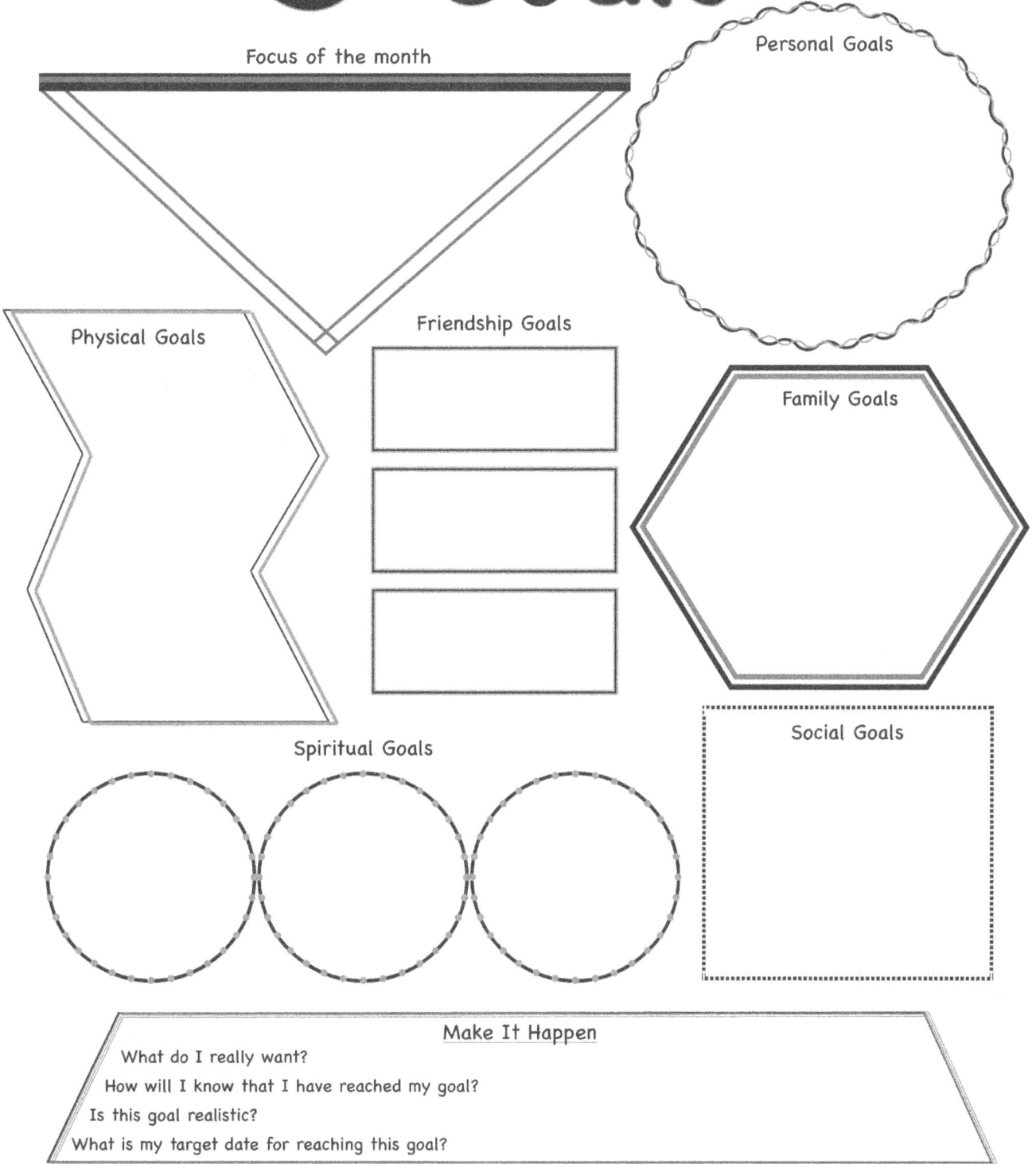

Taking It Home
Toward Yourself... Questions to take to my heart:

> Look into your heart as you answer these questions. This is introspection time — time to grapple with what drives your thinking and behavior. Be sure to "capture your thoughts."

Even though you would never have chosen for your parents to have divorced, do you think there are some ways in which you are a better person because of it? If so, what are they?

Do you think that because of what you have experienced with your parents' separation, you have learned any positive things that could impact your future? If so, what are they?

Do you think you are closer to either your mom or dad because of the divorce? If so, in what ways?

How are you doing on your goals this week?

Week 11

Taking It Home

Toward Others... Questions to take to others:

> Healing cannot become complete without affecting the lives of those around us. Be courageous and go outside your comfort zone to take a risk and work on your relationships with others. This is application time — time to take what you have learned and apply it to your individual experience.

Do you need to find a group of new Christian friends who will support you in this healing process?

When things get rough again, do you have someone in mind to whom you can turn? If so, who? If not, who can you think of?

How does your parents' divorce affect your own personal dating relationships?

What do you do when you see your parents making bad choices? Can you still respect your parents, knowing that they make mistakes?

Week 11

Taking It Home

Toward God... Questions to take to God:

> When you ask God a question, expect His Spirit to respond to your heart. Be careful not to rush it, or manufacture an answer. Don't jot down your idea of the "right answer." Just pose the question to God, and wait on Him to speak personally to your heart.

Have you allowed God to help you with your pain, or have you been refusing to let Him do so? If not, what is holding you back?

Do you have a scheduled devotional time each day? If not, make a commitment to start now.

How is your prayer life? Do you need to pump it up a bit?

Is improving your relationship with God one of your primary goals? If not, consider making it one now.

Week 11

Hope on the Horizon

Lesson Twelve
Week 12

GOALS

This week we want to:
1. Have fun
2. Appreciate and show gratitude to group attendees
3. Find ways to develop an "Attitude of Gratitude"
4. Define your own future
5. Consider future relationships
6. Elevate your relationship with Christ
7. Review the "Taking It Home" assignments
8. Celebrate your success

Verses of the week:

"I do all this for the sake of the gospel, that I may share in its blessings."

1 Corinthians 9:23

Be Blessed!

*"For I know the plans I have for you," declares the L*ord*, "plans to prosper you and not to harm you, plans to give you hope and a future."*

Jeremiah 29:11

SOMETHING TO THINK ABOUT

Congratulations! You stuck with it, and here we are twelve weeks later! It is hard to believe how much we have covered over the past few months. We hope you have learned a lot and have gained some new friendships. Everything we have talked about has been leading us to our goal: a future full of new possibilities. We hope you can take what you have learned and enjoy a full life of hope and promise. That is what these sessions have been all about: you and your future. Embrace the possibilities, and continue making steps toward them daily.

Plan today for a better tomorrow. Your future is in your hands.
Believe—Hope—Live!

Gratitude Check

What relationships are you the most grateful for?

What happened today that you are thankful for?

Think about your home. What about it are you grateful for?

I am thankful for my friendship with _____
  because _____
  _____.

I am grateful for who I am because _____.

Think about your abilities and talents. Which one do you appreciate the most?

I am grateful for my family because _____.

In what ways are you especially blessed?

Think about the experience of your parents' divorce. What is one thing you learned from it?

Something silly that I am grateful for is _____.

One of the things I am grateful to God for is _____.

Something at school that I am thankful for is _____.

What is something about your mom that makes you grateful?

What is something about your dad that makes you grateful?

Gratitude Journal

Daily Gratitude List
List at least four things you were grateful for today.

1.

2.

3.

4.

Lessons Learned from Challenges
List three challenging situations or people in your life and what good you're learning through each one.

1. I'm Learning:

2. I'm Learning:

3. I'm Learning:

People I am Thankful For
List five people who have made your life a little happier today.

1.

2.

3.

4.

5.

Best Part of My Day
Choose one moment of your day that made you happy and focus on it for five minutes.

Gratitude Journal

Daily Gratitude List
List at least four things you were grateful for today.

1.

2.

3.

4.

Lessons Learned from Challenges
List three challenging situations or people in your life and what good you're learning through each one.

1. I'm Learning:

2. I'm Learning:

3. I'm Learning:

People I am Thankful For
List five people who have made your life a little happier today.

1.

2.

3.

4.

5.

Best Part of My Day
Choose one moment of your day that made you happy and focus on it for five minutes.

Gratitude Journal

Daily Gratitude List
List at least four things you were grateful for today.

1.
2.
3.
4.

Lessons Learned from Challenges
List three challenging situations or people in your life and what good you're learning through each one.

1. I'm Learning:
2. I'm Learning:
3. I'm Learning:

People I am Thankful For
List five people who have made your life a little happier today.

1.
2.
3.
4.
5.

Best Part of My Day
Choose one moment of your day that made you happy and focus on it for five minutes.

Healthy Relationship Thoughts

1. To me, a healthy relationship means:

2. What qualities do I need to develop to be ready for a healthy relationship?

3. What are possible roadblocks for establishing a healthy relationship?

Characteristics	What do I bring into a healthy relationship?	What do I look for?
Physical Features		
Purpose/Drive		
Sensitive/Emotional		
Creative/Passions		
Spirituality		
Servant-Leader		
Interests/Hobbies		
Career/Financial		

Story About Me

What is your first memory as a child?

What do you remember about your family before the separation?

What is your favorite memory of your family before the divorce?

What do you remember about the time you found out about the divorce?

What was the hardest thing to get used to in a single-parent home?

What do you remember about missing the other parent?

What do you miss most about living with both parents?

What have you learned through your parents' relationship?

How will you try to do things differently in your own relationship someday?

What things would you do the same in your own relationship?

What have you learned through this experience that you will bring with you into your own future family?

Praying for your Future Spouse

Relationship with God

PRAY...

That they are a believer
That their faith would grow stronger
That they will stand firm in their beliefs
That they feel God's presence and guidance
For strength to overcome sin issues
For God's peace in times of difficulty
To resist temptation

Relationship with Others

PRAY...

That they will make good, sound choices
That they would be an example to others
For good, solid same-faith friendships
For safety and protection
That they would sustain peer pressure
For purity in their relationships

Relationship with Family

PRAY....

For godly examples for them to follow
For protection for their loved ones
To have forgiveness modeled in their home
For honesty and integrity to be valued
That love would be in their home
For healthy relationships

Dear Future Spouse,

Love,

Taking It Home

Toward Yourself... Questions to take to my heart:

> Look into your heart as you answer these questions. This is introspection time — time to grapple with what drives your thinking and behavior. Be sure to "capture your thoughts."

What are the main reasons people get married? Divorced?

What are the most important qualities you look for in a wife/husband? Are they the same when looking for a boyfriend/girlfriend?

What do you think you can do to avoid having your own future marriage end in divorce?

In what ways do you think you will be a better parent than your own parents?

What hopes and dreams do you have for your own future?

Week 12

Taking It Home

Toward Others... Questions to take to others:

> Healing cannot become complete without affecting the lives of those around us. Be courageous and go outside your comfort zone to take a risk and work on your relationships with others. This is application time — time to take what you have learned and apply it to your own individual experience.

What are some of the positive aspects of your parents' divorce?

What are some things you have learned through this journey?

How do you intend on protecting your own relationships in your future?

Share with your parents three good things that have happened in your life as a result of their divorce.

1. _____
2. _____
3. _____

Week 12

Taking It Home

Toward God... Questions to take to God:

> When you ask God a question, expect His Spirit to respond to your heart. Be careful not to rush it, or manufacture an answer. Don't jot down your idea of the "right answer." Just pose the question to God, and wait on Him to speak personally to your heart.

Why do you think God allows divorce to happen?

What has God taught you through your parent's divorce?

What role will God have in your future? Your future marriage? Your future family?

Are you closer to God now than you were before the separation? How do you plan on continuing to grow spiritually?

Week 12

CONGRATULATIONS!

HAS SUCCESSFULLY COMPLETED

THE JOURNEY

"For I know the plans I have for you," declares the LORD, "plans to prosper you and not to harm you, plans to give you hope and a future."
- Jeremiah 29:11

_____
Leader Signature   Date

_____
Attendee Signature   Date

www.ingramcontent.com/pod-product-compliance
Lightning Source LLC
Chambersburg PA
CBHW080548170426
43195CB00016B/2710